WHAT OTHERS

"Those looking for a road map for life can get directions from the Bishops.... The co-authors, who are volunteer coaches for TheHopeLine, share stories and insights cleverly separated into six thematic sections.... The book incorporates faith without unnecessary preaching." (For full review, see http://publishersweekly.com/978-0-9856-2486-6.)
Publishers Weekly

"Packed with zest, adventure, and love, *Wheels of Wisdom* offers an unusual combination of joyous living and an appeal to grab each moment and make it count. A great read for those who enjoy a virtual trip with some intriguing insights."
LISA LICKEL, author of *The Last Detail*

"I found myself pulled into the stories and jealous of the rich life lessons Tim and Debbie were experiencing. Seeing the beauty in nature, taking time to know our unique calling, asking for help, and being in a position to expect a miracle are things we often miss in our routine, safe lives. *Wheels of Wisdom* is a wonderful story of adventure, filled with romance, humor, insights, and a reminder that we are all privileged travelers in this world of wonder."
DAN MILLER, *New York Times* best-selling author of *48 Days to the Work You Love*

"*Wheels of Wisdom* offers the unique combination of being extremely readable and thought-provoking at the same time. Sharing in Tim and Debbie's adventures leads one to consider how matters of everyday faith, preparation, decision-making, and perspective affect us not only in the moment, but throughout our lives."
DR. JOHN GIANNINI, head men's basketball coach at La Salle University

"If you want to enjoy an engaging read while also being challenged to think about things bigger than yourself and beyond the next moment, then you've opened the right book."
DAVE ANDERSON, Director of Rescue for TheHopeLine

"I love the practical nature of this book. It has a great design, easy readability—it's excellent! *Wheels of Wisdom* makes a wonderful devotional to do on your own or with a friend or small group."
CONSTANCE RHODES, founder and CEO of FINDING*balance*, Inc.

"Tim and Debbie Bishop know better than just about anyone the power of bicycle travel—for the body and soul. As with their other cycling chronicles, *Wheels of Wisdom* offers plenty of sage advice for people at all stages of life and people who might turn to a trusty bicycle to help them make the next big transition. Whether you're a beginner or veteran cyclist, this book has something for you."
JIM SAYER, Executive Director of Adventure Cycling Association

"It was a privilege to ride along the roads of life with the Bishops in *Wheels of Wisdom*! Their view of the world on two wheels gave a unique perspective of how God makes His presence known."
STACEY LOUISO-HENRY, author, editor, and worship artist at writingdownlife.com

"Inspiring, entertaining, and authentic, *Wheels of Wisdom* contains great lessons for anyone who is searching for answers to life's questions."
KOLINDA KING DUER, holistic health counselor, author, and singer/songwriter from College Grove, Tennessee

"Thanks to *Wheels of Wisdom*, I vicariously enjoyed a bicycle tour without the blisters and the sore back. Tim and Debbie Bishop took me to states I never visited and showed me sights I'd never seen. I learned about God and myself. What a great adventure!"
PETER DEHAAN, author and blogger at PeterDeHaan.com

"Generous, kind, and caring: that's how the Bishops live their lives. This book is infused with those wonderful traits. Not only are Tim and Debbie determined to grow through every experience and adventure in their lives, but they humbly share those lessons with us as if we were sitting across the kitchen table from them."
TIM ALTMAN, CEO of the Dawson McAllister Association and TheHopeLine

"Charming townspeople, beautiful scenery, and exciting adventures set the stage for powerful life lessons in *Wheels of Wisdom*."
CHRISTIE HAGERMAN, youth advocate, blogger, and former triathlete from Easley, South Carolina

"If you have questions and concerns about your life, your relationships, and God, then read *Wheels of Wisdom*. It may change your outlook, answer some of your questions, and give you hope for a more meaningful life."
TOM NENADAL, owner of Back from the Past Bicycles in Marshall, Missouri

"*Wheels of Wisdom* captures some memorable experiences from the Bishops' bicycling trips across America and intertwines those experiences with thought-provoking, impactful insights on living life with purpose and meaning. The authors present their life lessons with sincerity and conviction yet without being 'preachy.' I highly recommend this enjoyable book for readers of all ages who want to improve their lives or reignite their passion for life."
TIMOTHY STREETER, IT lead analyst from Fulton, New York

"Descriptive, passionate, and thought-provoking, *Wheels of Wisdom* will encourage and challenge readers with life-building lessons. I highly recommend this book for anyone who enjoys adventure, cycling, achieving goals, and finding hope for their lives."
LANCE BARRY, call center manager and avid cyclist from Sioux Falls, South Dakota

"In *Wheels of Wisdom*, Tim and Debbie Bishop share more than a love of cross-country cycling. They share a keen eye on life, philosophical reflections of trying experiences, and the valuable spiritual lessons they learned along the way. Travel along. When the ride stops, you'll be different."
HEATHER RANDALL, CEO of Christian Women Affiliate

"Tim and Debbie Bishop's 'up close and personal' stories will delight you and make you gasp, smile, and grow misty-eyed as you explore America—and your own life—from the seat of a bicycle. This book will challenge, inspire, and encourage you."
PATTI SMITH, executive administrative assistant from Milford, Ohio

"A refreshing read packed full of practical life lessons, *Wheels of Wisdom*, with its down-to-earth style, paints a fascinating picture of the cycling adventures of Tim and Debbie Bishop. Wherever you are in faith, this book asks soul-searching questions. Whether it is a life, relationship, or spiritual question, the Bishops share their answers gently and authentically and point to the source of all wisdom—God Himself."
KAREN BRITS, housewife and mother from Northborough, Massachusetts

"Tim and Debbie Bishop share God's love and teachings through stories from their cross-country trips by bicycle. *Wheels of Wisdom* is a truly unique and exciting book that aims to make us all better people."
TIM MALIKOWSKI, accounting professional from Hampden, Maine

"We're all travelers on a life journey and need help every now and then. Learn from this couple while you're dreaming of new adventures, pondering about past travels, and living in the here and now. Inspiring, confronting, and uplifting!"
HENK-JAN VAN DER KLIS, project manager from Balkbrug, The Netherlands

"Stories in *Wheels of Wisdom* will inspire, encourage, and challenge you. The Bishops share openly their ups and downs, and teach, by example, how to apply one's faith to everyday circumstances. Reading this book could be a life-changing experience for you whether you're a cyclist or not."
KEN SHIRK, tax professional and avid bicycle tourist from Lebanon, Pennsylvania

Inspiration for Your Own Adventure

TIM & DEBBIE BISHOP

WHEELS OF
Wisdom
LIFE LESSONS FOR THE RESTLESS SPIRIT

OPEN
ROAD
PRESS

Publisher's Note

Certain portions of this text retell stories that originally appeared in *Two Are Better*, which is a memoir also published by Open Road Press and written by the same authors. Whereas *Two Are Better* communicates a life story, *Wheels of Wisdom* emphasizes life lessons learned from the Bishops' three long-distance bicycle tours. Any duplicate accounts presented in this publication are for the purpose of instruction and personal application.

This publication is designed to teach, enlighten, and inspire. There is no guarantee that the hyperlinks will work as intended. The publisher is not responsible for viruses, malware, or other computer scripts that may alter or destroy computer data. Readers who click on hyperlinks do so at their own risk.

Published in Thompson's Station, Tennessee, USA by Open Road Press.
www.openroadpress.com
First Edition

Scripture taken from the New King James Version®.
Copyright © 1982 by Thomas Nelson, Inc.
Used by permission. All rights reserved.

Library of Congress Control Number: 2015917683
Print Edition ISBN: 978-0-9856248-6-6
Photo-enhanced e-book ISBN: 978-0-9856248-4-2

Front cover design by Micah Kandros
Interior design of print edition by GKS Creative
Preliminary manuscript evaluation by Erin Casey
Copyediting by Kevin Miller
Proofreading by John David Kudrick

TheHopeLine®, as referred to in this book, is a registered trademark of The Shepherd's Call, Inc.

CONTENTS

FOREWORD

Everyone is looking for insight into life's challenges. We all want to know how to achieve victories, but we also want to know how to overcome defeats and deal with agonizing heartaches—or avoid them altogether. At some point, we all wonder: *What is the best way to navigate this voyage we call life?* If we hope to find peace, satisfaction, and the encouragement to sail forward with purpose, we need to pack the right supplies.

Certainly, you don't want to begin a trek across the open frontier, whether by bicycle or on foot, without the bare necessities: a compass, food, water, and protection from the elements. However, you may also want to consider packing wisdom, encouragement, perseverance, and hope. Wisdom will help you make good decisions, encouragement will sustain you, and perseverance will keep you moving forward. Hope seals the success of a journey across any frontier, because it convinces you that safe arrival at your destination is possible. You'll find bare necessities like these in the pages that follow. It's wise to include them on your list of supplies for any adventure through life.

As Director of Rescue for TheHopeLine, I have the opportunity to serve and oversee others who serve many people who lack these bare necessities and are struggling to move forward. Each year, TheHopeLine engages tens of thousands of people around the globe. In my role, I've learned three things about the need out there: First, people are struggling regardless of location, age, occupation, ethnicity, religion, or income. Second, everyone needs help sometimes. No one is immune to heartache, temptation, poor decisions, or difficult circumstances. Finally, there truly is hope—real hope—for every problem life throws our way. Hurdling those obstacles requires doing something different. Simply wishing things will get better or expecting we can make changes without significant effort won't bring about the lasting change we seek.

I've seen Debbie and Tim Bishop serve diligently as volunteer Hope Coaches on TheHopeLine since they got married a few years ago. The Bishops know what it takes to come alongside people, listen to them, and encourage them to make some of the changes to which I alluded above. In this book, you're going to see that they also know how to present wisdom and truth in a unique and engaging manner, one that will allow you to digest what these lessons mean for your own life.

As I have gotten to know the Bishops and observed the bicycle trekking they love, I have found them to be both intriguing and a little crazy at the same time. After all, what kind of people would subject their old rear ends to such abuse? I mean, come on, they must be kidding…bicycling thousands of miles cross-country in their fifties? Yet what became clear to me is that they have experiences gained both on their bicycles and by way of their personal journeys through life that bring great learning opportunities to their readers. Their experiences teach lessons of wisdom, love, fear, disappointment, and victory. It's not surprising to me that they are writers. Tim, skilled in the details of finance, sees the nuances of each day, mile, and bend in the road. Debbie, an educator by trade, is gifted at telling stories. She articulates them with emotion, humor, candor, and compassion. Together, they weave their lessons into concise tidbits of truth that are both compelling and rich in application.

Regardless of your background, beliefs, or interest in travel by bicycle, you will enjoy this book. It's neither a theological book nor an adventure journal, though it contains elements of both. More importantly, it is a book you can relate to. You'll find insights into some important life truths as you look in on the Bishops' moments of excitement, joy, disappointment, perseverance, and physical challenge. This book will stimulate some thought about your own life. If you want some inspiration and some fun, a fresh take on common sense, and some ideas for self-improvement, then read on.

Better yet, don't just read this book; apply it. Consider the questions at the end of each lesson and implement what you learn. I think you'll find, as I have, that there's always room for personal improvement. What better way to roll forward than with *Wheels of Wisdom*? So, dive into the entertaining and motivating lessons that follow. You're going to appreciate this journey immensely.

Dave Anderson
Director of Rescue for TheHopeLine

INTRODUCTION

Have you ever seen two bicycles on the side of a road loaded down with gear for what seemed like a long trip? If you saw a middle-aged man and woman beside those bicycles looking at a map and trying to find their way, that could have been us! We're Tim and Debbie Bishop, and we've discovered some fantastic things on our travels that we'd love to share with you.

After many years of being single, we've discovered bicycle touring to be an incredible way to bond with each other while also learning about life and ourselves. Even though we travel by ourselves to maximize the experience, we're all about sharing the adventures we've undertaken since marrying in June 2010. Rather than inviting others to come along with us, we've found a better way to share our experiences. You're about to discover that method firsthand as you dig deeper into this book.

A bicycle tour offers the freedom of the open road, beautiful scenery, and a personal challenge. However, far more life changing are the lessons learned on the road. This open-air classroom captivates one's undivided attention, which provides an effective forum to communicate profound truths to those who choose to listen. We've found it's easier to learn when God has our attention.

God? This seems like a good opportunity to allay any concerns that invoking the name of God might raise and to explain who will likely enjoy this book. First, this isn't another one of those books about a long-distance bicycle tour, as good—or bad—as some of those books are. Sure, every lesson we share oozes with the adventure of a bicycle tour to parts unknown, but this is really an inspirational and motivational book about life. It contains practical wisdom while also touching on spiritual truth. We designed it specifically for those who are looking to get more out of life.

We come at life from a Christian perspective. That's just who we are, and we can't very well be who we aren't. We know that not all people are in the same place in their spiritual journey— or even believe such a thing exists. Nevertheless, we think the experiences we relate in this book will resonate with people who are curious about spiritual matters, or who simply enjoy adventure and are interested in what adventures can teach us about ourselves and about life. We encourage you to keep an open mind about what you might glean and to prepare for an unusual ride, the likes of which you might never have experienced. In short, we respect where you're coming from, and we humbly request that you do the same for us. We're sincere people who like to share from the heart.

Bicycling across the country isn't for everyone, and that's okay. Even if you'd rather relax in a recliner than strap on a helmet and pedal sixty miles a day, we think you'll enjoy the adventures and lessons we share in this book. You'll end each ride without saddle sores and tired muscles, but we can't guarantee your journey with us will be pain free. You're bound to experience some growing pains whether or not you're prepared for remedial action. Nevertheless, the beauty of the road and the fruit of self-examination are worth it.

The stories in *Wheels of Wisdom* come from three long-distance tours. Our "honeymoon on wheels" occurred in the summer of 2010 shortly after we married. We were first-time newlyweds at age fifty-two. We've shared this journey in our inaugural book, *Two Are Better: Midlife Newlyweds Bicycle Coast to Coast,* a memoir that describes how God brought us together and then the celebration that followed on our self-supported tour from Oregon to Maine. Marriage was not the only thing new to us then. Neither of us had ever toured overnight by bicycle. We had much to learn about marriage and life (and we still do!), and you'll benefit from some of those lessons in this book.

Our first tour whetted our appetites for more adventure. In 2012, we cycled from Florida to Maine on our Mom-to-Mom Tour. It was not only convenient, but also meaningful to start and end a tour where each of our mothers lived while enjoying America's Atlantic coast in between.

Then, in 2014, we embarked across America yet again when we cycled from Oregon to Pennsylvania. We dedicated that tour to raising awareness and funds for a cause that is dear to our hearts. Hence, the name *TheHopeLine Tour of 2014* came to be. Our sights were set on Rhode Island, but we needed to alter our plans, as you will learn later in the book.

In total, we've toured over ten thousand miles. You can pack many lessons into that distance.

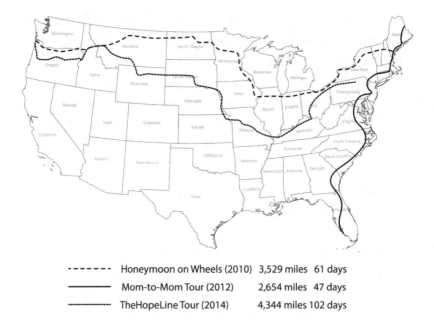

------- Honeymoon on Wheels (2010)   3,529 miles 61 days
———— Mom-to-Mom Tour (2012)   2,654 miles 47 days
·············· TheHopeLine Tour (2014)   4,344 miles 102 days

The Bishops' routes

While you'll enjoy more pictures about each lesson in the photo-enhanced e-book version of *Wheels of Wisdom,* we have many more photos and even some videos at www.openroadpress .com. Regardless of the version you are reading, you may want to keep a pencil and some paper handy as you consider the personal reflection questions at the end of each lesson.

Now, without further ado, it's time to get moving, to pass on some wisdom from our lives to you while having some fun along the way. We're glad you're along for the ride. You'll miss too much if you stay home.

SECTION

I

Charting the Course

We'll be sharing some lessons in this section that speak directly to the need to recognize your purpose and calling, to make necessary if not courageous choices, and to adopt a refreshing attitude that acknowledges the right way to do things. Discerning right from wrong is important, but it's not always easy. We hope the following lessons will help enlighten your path.

SECTION I TAKEAWAYS
Things to Consider

1. _____

_____

_____

2. _____

_____

_____

3. _____

_____

_____

4. _____

_____

_____

5. _____

_____

_____

LESSON 1

What Were You Made For?

All of us were created with unique qualities, and we were not cut out for just anything. If you were made for the goals you pursue, the satisfaction and energy you gain from your daily activities will confirm your calling.

BY DEBBIE

Somewhere in the Midwest on TheHopeLine Tour—it might have been Iowa or Nebraska—Tim stated something that has stuck with me ever since. After I had exclaimed how much I loved the tour we were on, Tim looked at me and said, "We were made for this."

I'll never forget that. Tim is like E. F. Hutton. When he talks, people listen—probably because he thinks before he opens his mouth. I love that about him. Truly wise is a person who thinks before he speaks and says something that sticks with you.

A few weeks later, Tim's statement came to life. I was made for days like day seventy-six of TheHopeLine Tour. The cool weather, intermittent sun, rolling hills, and beautiful scenery invigorated me. Mile after mile, I felt my burning muscles and the fresh air in my lungs. I was made for that. Not only did we relish a good dose of bicycling, we climbed up and down eight flights of stairs to the top of a fire tower to catch a breathtaking view of the vast Missouri landscape. It was a picture-perfect day. After a rest day and much sleep the night before to recover from a grueling stretch in the Ozarks, I had sprung back to my energetic self once again.

Made for this!

I'm amazed at how difficult that bike tour was and how long we'd been gone. Since we'd departed from the Oregon coast well over two months earlier, I'd had a cortisone shot in my knee, burned my foot with boiling water while camping, and been diagnosed with an overuse injury known as "chronic compartment syndrome," which kept me off the bike for two weeks. There we were on day seventy-six, approaching Cape Girardeau, Missouri, and the Mississippi River in mid-September, with many miles left to ride.

Nevertheless, I was made for physical exertion and adventures like that. My knee, foot, and leg had all healed. And so we carried on. Some people might think I should have had my head examined to determine what kept me going after all those issues on the road. Once again, though, I was made for that. Just because we had a few setbacks along the way didn't mean we should have stopped and given up.

If you are doing something you were made to do, you naturally want to venture forward in that made-for-you task you love. Even when hardships come, you persevere, because that is part of the process.

Not all of us are wired to bicycle seventy miles a day. For that matter, not all of us are designed to work outdoors in the winter, to practice law or medicine, to spend a lot of time in front of a camera, or to work with children. Have you ever asked yourself, *What was I made to do?* The answer to that question could change your life. We all have unique gifts and desires. Once you discover your special attributes and devote your time to utilizing them, you'll experience deep joy and fulfillment as you live out a facet of God's calling on your life.

For I know the thoughts that I think toward you, says the Lord, thoughts of peace and not of evil, to give you a future and a hope.
JEREMIAH 29:11

Personal REFLECTION:

1. What are your strongest personal attributes? What subjects interest you most?

2. How are you applying your strengths and interests on a daily basis?

3. When you think about what you need to accomplish today, do you feel energized or exhausted? Activities you were made to do should energize you no matter how difficult they seem.

LESSON 2

Perfect Circumstances Never Arrive

You cannot wait for optimal circumstances before moving forward. Nor can you allow discouraging circumstances to deter you. Your opportunity may have a short lifespan.

BY TIM

I love lessons that come to us when we least expect them. Sometimes, you experience these moments merely by observing another person.

On our honeymoon on wheels tour, we enjoyed two nights at a beautiful cabin on the shore of Petenwell Lake in Wisconsin with our host and friend Mike Porter and his family. Then, Mike drove Debbie and me several hours through violent thunderstorms to return us to our route. He dropped us into Cascade, Iowa, under sunny skies. Life was good! After breaking bread with Mike at a local Subway, we resumed our southerly journey to avoid Lake Michigan and the metropolitan Chicago area.

Less than two hours into our ride, we noticed a solo cyclist approaching on a recumbent bicycle with a trailer in tow. Given our late start and our goal of making it to the Mississippi River crossing at

Muscatine, Iowa, before nightfall, we didn't want to stop for a break already. However, our polite waves would not prevent the upcoming conversation.

"Hi! Where are you headed to?" our fellow traveler shouted as he slowed his bicycle and crossed over to our side of the road, as if to pin us next to the shoulder. His maneuver made it difficult for us to cycle past him. We were anxious to continue our ride, but we weren't inclined to be downright rude. This fellow obviously wanted to talk.

"We're headed toward the East Coast," Debbie said. "We started in Oregon on July third."

"I'm headed to the Pacific Ocean," he replied. "I've had eight flats, and I've had to replace my rear rim twice. However, I'm not about to stop."

Soon, we discovered his name was Jim. He sold cars for a living in Hendersonville, Tennessee, where Debbie's father used to live. We had been there the prior summer to help her dad move to Denver.

"I've always wanted to do this but couldn't swing the schedule—until this year," Jim said. "My wife isn't much into bicycling, so I decided to go it alone."

Deep within, I felt the contrast taking shape. I might have been in Jim's shoes had I not met Debbie, although I'm doubtful I would have undertaken such a daunting challenge as cycling across America alone. After thirty-odd years as a single adult, I'd had enough loneliness. Maybe this guy just wanted a break from his wife—or vice versa. However, I couldn't help but replay the following life truth over and over in my head: *It is not good for man to be alone.* I also thought about how fortunate Debbie and I had been. We'd only had one flat tire and one issue with a screw coming loose from the rear rack on Debbie's bicycle. Ours had been a pleasure ride compared to Jim's journey. Yet he had an undeniable determination.

As Jim continued to bend our ears, we sensed he needed to engage with someone, and we were the logical choice on that road with little traffic, few homes, and no pedestrians. He was lonely, and why wouldn't he be after countless hours of solitary cycling and camping? Eventually, Jim had his fill of conversation and realized that we all needed to move on to maximize the daylight.

After parting ways with Jim, Debbie and I talked about how blessed we felt to have one another—and to have experienced so few mechanical issues on our journey. We marveled at Jim's determination and wondered whether either of us had the gumption to accomplish solo what it appeared Jim would do, although he had much climbing ahead of him. While we understood the type of experience he would have in the northern plains and the Pacific Northwest, we felt sorry for him that he wouldn't be enjoying it with someone special by his side. It was hard for us to imagine an adventure like ours without each other. We both concluded we wouldn't have considered cycling across the country alone.

As we continued cycling through the beautiful bounty of Iowa's cornfields, however, we began to see another side to Jim's situation. Debbie and I had lived very full single lives before meeting one another and marrying. Feeling sorry for ourselves and avoiding great experiences because we were single would have made no sense. To the contrary, we'd had ample time and resources as singles. We also did not shoulder the significant responsibilities associated with raising children, which might have prevented us from pursuing many enjoyable activities that helped develop us as individuals. We had matured the single way while our married-with-children peers were learning and growing through the rigors and sacrifices needed to raise families.

Although the grass may always seem greener on the other side, it isn't. The grass is simply a different type. The magnificent abundance that surrounded us on the rolling hills of Iowa, as well as the unforgettable images of cycling through the Pacific Northwest, reminded us that Jim's journey would dazzle him despite his solitude.

Any of life's circumstances comes with its own benefits. If you recognize your advantages rather than dwelling on the negatives, you'll be in a better position to recognize—and seize—your opportunities. Allowing a pessimistic perception of your circumstances to dictate your pursuits, however, will quash them. If God has placed a dream deep within your heart, eventually you'll have an opportunity to chase it. Look for opportunities in every situation. Ideal circumstances will never come, so don't wait for them.

> **He who observes the wind will not sow,**
> **and he who regards the clouds will not reap.**
>
> ECCLESIASTES 11:4

Personal REFLECTION:

1. What are you putting off because you don't think the time is right?

2. Can you think of someone who seems to have it better than you? Think of an advantage you have that they don't.

3. What steps can you take now to move closer to what you'd like to accomplish?

LESSON 3

Blow the Whistle

Packing a positive attitude for your pursuit will always
make it more pleasurable and satisfying. Establishing
some accountability will help you stay on track.

BY DEBBIE

W hen you are touring by bicycle, you never know what to
expect when setting out each morning. All you know is
that you will encounter something new and interesting,
and perhaps learn something in the process. On one particular day
during TheHopeLine Tour, we would encounter another new state and
learn a trick to becoming a better person.

Despite a cool and overcast start, we had wonderful weather for the
remainder of the day. An early-morning race with a pair of deer proved
too much for us, yet we persevered for our third consecutive day of
biking more than seventy miles.

Leaving Metropolis, Illinois, and cycling into Kentucky all in one
day felt like quite an accomplishment. For some reason, I thought Illinois
would be flat, but it isn't. We climbed up and down hills until we stopped

for lunch at mile forty-one. We also switched maps, leaving the Great Rivers South map and heading in the direction of the Underground Railroad route. Our new route and new direction foreshadowed a change I would make later in the day to improve our travel experience.

The end of our time in Illinois came at Cave-in-Rock, where we caught a ride on the free ferry across the Ohio River. No cars accompanied us on the ferry, just the two guys who operated the boat. As soon as we entered Kentucky, nothing awaited us except more hills—no people, no homes, and no crops for miles. Just like in other states along TheHopeLine Tour, we had the place to ourselves. The hilly terrain meant we had some challenging climbs, while the dense forest with no people around made for a lengthy and uncertain ride to civilization.

In our travels, we've used maps published by a nonprofit bicycle-touring advocate called the Adventure Cycling Association (www .adventurecycling.org). Those maps mentioned the possibility of loose dogs in Kentucky, so Tim had a bright orange whistle hanging from his neck, and I had one in the outside pocket of my handlebar bag for easy access. Mine offered the added benefits of serving as a compass and a thermometer. I had used the thermometer and compass more than the whistle, but I must admit I loved blowing the whistle on dogs that chased us.

At that time on TheHopeLine Tour, we'd already had to blow the whistle on dogs in Missouri and Illinois. I can remember thinking, *Kentucky dogs: be prepared! We won't be wasting our precious water squirting you or fending you off with our bicycle pumps.* The whistle would be the way to ward off unwanted canines in pursuit.

Before encountering any loose dogs, however, I discovered another use for the whistle, but you need the assistance of a spouse or a friend. I'm talking about breaking a bad habit I'd had at times on that trip... well, actually, two bad habits.

It all started on the prior day when I'd made a sarcastic comment and Tim blew the whistle as a referee would and shouted, "Unnecessary sarcasm, fifteen yards!" He was joking, of course. However, after entering Kentucky, I thought, *What a great way to break a habit!*

So, I said to him, "If I complain about anything for the rest of the day, I want you to blow the whistle on me."

It may sound strange, but my request for Tim to hold me accountable kept my grumbling in check. I set goals for myself every day, and many days, I pray that I will not complain. Day after day, I fall short. On that particular day, I thought blowing the whistle on my complaining would be a great way to break that horrible habit. And it worked!

Instead of complaining to Tim, I started thinking of ways to put a positive spin on things. My knee hurt, but instead of complaining about it, I thought about the beautiful sky. I was so sick of the endless hills, but instead of dwelling on it by talking about it, I said I was grateful for the lack of traffic on those hills! The fear of the whistle blowing with each complaint kept me from whining. I tested Tim while pedaling up a very steep hill and complained about it. Sure enough, he blew the whistle!

If you have a bad habit to break, ask someone to "blow the whistle" every time you indulge in that habit. The list of habits that could benefit from some whistle-blowing interference includes gossiping, complaining, swearing, being late, smoking…the list is endless. Chances are this behavior-modification plan will get you into shape rather quickly. You will be "a better you" once you've broken the bad habit and replaced it with a new, healthier one. Instead of complaining, turn it into gratitude. No one will blow the whistle on you if you're grateful and full of joy!

Thirty-two miles into Kentucky, we ran out of sun. Yet we were glad to have entered state number eleven on TheHopeLine Tour. After climbing 4,700 feet of elevation, we were heartened when a woman at a convenience store in Sturgis reserved a motel room for us. The map listed none, but she knew of a place with cabins for rent. They had closed early, but she had an "in" and, therefore, so did we. Small-town Kentucky hospitality was in the air.

When we arrived at the cabin, we had more pleasant surprises: it was beautiful, the price was right, and the adjoining market packed us a home-cooked meal—which goes to show that when you stop complaining, things will work out well in the end!

Attitude. It has so much influence on the success of a journey and the fulfillment of a destiny—and whether you will be miserable or happy along the way. Make sure you check your attitude at the door to your pursuit.

Whatever things are true, whatever things are noble, whatever things are just, whatever things are pure, whatever things are lovely, whatever things are of good report, if there is any virtue and if there is anything praiseworthy—meditate on these things.

PHILIPPIANS 4:8

Personal REFLECTION:

1. Which bad habit would you like to "blow the whistle" on?

2. Can you think of anyone who could help hold you accountable in overcoming this bad habit?

3. Which is more agonizing: continuing to struggle with the bad habit or giving permission to a trusted individual to help you stop it?

LESSON 4

History Does Not Always Repeat Itself

When you are choosing a path forward, don't assume
what happened yesterday will repeat itself today. Often,
it does not. Past setbacks can hamper your progress,
if you let them.

BY TIM

Wild Wyoming weather on the previous day had us second-guessing ourselves on the thirty-fifth day of TheHopeLine Tour. On our way to Newcastle, another early-afternoon buildup of dark, billowy clouds thwarted our efforts for a sixty-plus-mile day and entry into South Dakota. Given the lengthy service-less leg that awaited us, we holed up at a local Subway to see if the skies would clear. They did not. Hence, we scurried around in late afternoon for shelter from the impending storm. We were disappointed, as we had more miles in us and a church in Custer, South Dakota, ready to host us for the evening.

The prior day's tempestuous weather had intimidated us into staying put. Our vivid recollection of perilously close lightning strikes and driving rain made it hard to imagine subjecting ourselves to those elements again, even though there was no guarantee of a repeat performance. Dark clouds looming in the shadow of our frightful flight to safety helped cast a decision that seemed wrong by the end of the day. The clouds came, but the storm did not...at least from where we sat.

Herd of pronghorn in Wyoming

Experience is an excellent teacher, but sometimes, it can get in the way. We ended up with a high rent rather than a free one. We also deferred forty-five miles of riding time. Maybe we avoided golf-ball-sized hailstones ten miles down the road or a journey into Custer using headlamps. Regardless, we wouldn't get anywhere standing still.

We embarked the following day, fully prepared for the road construction ahead, thanks to a good night's sleep. Wyoming had been very good to us despite the regular afternoon onslaught of black thunderheads and high winds. We liked the road conditions, the low traffic, and the scenery. If South Dakota offered those features and delivered calmer weather with more services, we would be in biker heaven.

Rumbling both on and above the road in Wyoming

Isn't it interesting how we are influenced by recent history, particularly when we've encountered setbacks? We see similar pessimistic tendencies from some of the people with whom we interact on TheHopeLine. Past troubles can make such an impact that a debilitating paralysis sets in and keeps them from moving forward in life. Yet just as all roads are not the same, neither are the unlimited scenarios that lie ahead in life. History does not always repeat itself—or, as they say in the investment world, "past performance is not necessarily indicative of future results."

There's a difference between being realistic and being negative. When your decision-making acknowledges all of the possibilities, not just those you'd like to prevent from happening again, you're being fair to the process. Debbie and I weren't apt to bog down too many more times on TheHopeLine Tour like we had on that day. We had too far yet to travel. There was more work to be done.

**No one, having put his hand to the plow,
and looking back, is fit for the kingdom of God.**

LUKE 9:62B

Personal REFLECTION:

1. Which negative experiences do you tend to dwell on?

2. Do you anticipate these same experiences will happen to you again?

3. Tell a close friend or relative about your fears so he or she can encourage you when negative thoughts threaten to take over.

LESSON 5

Road Map for Life

When you travel to parts unknown, you need a reliable
map. And when you feel you're losing your way through
life, it's time to consult the road map for life—and to
follow what it says.

BY DEBBIE

Francis Marion National Forest was the setting for a beautiful
ride on the Mom-to-Mom Tour after we left Moncks Corner,
South Carolina. Tall pine trees and plenty of underbrush on
both sides of the road made for tranquil touring. The prior evening's
thunderstorms had cooled the air. We cycled rain free, despite remnants
of early-morning showers in the rumble strips.

Exactly how we found our way through places like South Carolina's
"Low Country" bordered on the miraculous. We cycled for miles through
forested land and then turned onto another desolate road for many
more miles. Hours of cycling separated towns on our route. It was easy
to question whether we were lost.

Tim navigates phenomenally, but he is the first to admit he needs
effective tools to work with. When we decided to bicycle across the

country on our honeymoon, we knew we needed help to find our way. Neither of us had any experience with bicycle touring or the areas we would travel through. We talked to bike mechanics, recreational outfitters, and adventurers who had already bicycled across the United States. They provided much useful information.

Francis Marion National Forest in South Carolina

We were also delighted to find the turn-by-turn maps published by the Adventure Cycling Association (ACA). ACA's expert staff and years of exploration by bicycle have contributed to a superb set of maps at minimal cost. Those maps have led us across thousands of miles of scenic touring while steering us clear of danger spots and saving us time and money. Who wouldn't take advantage of a resource like that? It pays to consult the experts.

Even though we had invested in the best bicycling maps available, we'd been in such a harried pace with our wedding and trip planning that we hadn't studied the maps in advance. Once on the road, we were so intent on our surroundings and the experience itself that we neglected much of the detail on our maps. We didn't even understand the abundant capabilities on Tim's new GPS.

We only began to heed the detail on ACA's "power-packed" maps during our Mom-to-Mom Tour. Not only do they show where to go and how to get there, they list contact information for local accommodations, restaurants, bike shops, libraries, post offices, grocery and convenience stores, police stations, hospitals, and camping choices. Holding an ACA map on a bicycle tour is like clutching a security blanket as a child. Both instill comfort. Studying the maps made our touring experience far better and far easier than when we had first set out. We still had much to learn, which we would glean by paying more attention to the details on the maps.

Just as bicycle tourists want help for their adventures, most people are looking for guidance along this journey we call life. Recently, I Googled "self-help" and received 366 million results. How does one sift through the clutter to find help that really works?

For years, I assumed I would figure out life's challenges on my own. Self-help was my thing. Armed with a degree in psychology, I attended all kinds of self-help groups in the 1980s before I came to the end of my self-made road map to meaning...unfulfilled. I realized I couldn't create meaning and purpose by myself. In my "self-help mode," the Bible made no sense to me. It was like reading a road map upside down while driving seventy miles per hour in search of my destination.

When I became a Christian and finally allowed God to guide me through life, His Holy Spirit kindled my heart and stimulated my mind as I read the Bible. I could ask God to shed light on challenging passages. Studying the Bible with others has also helped illuminate its meaning for me.

Just like the bicycling maps, the Bible offers more information than I realized at first. It describes how to get along with others, how to make good decisions, and how to deal with all sorts of emotional pain, in addition to providing other practical help. No wonder it is the best-selling book in the world. The Bible has become my daily dose of wisdom, hope, and encouragement.

AAA maps, ACA maps, and GPS devices are all wonderful tools when you need help navigating from one location to another, but where do you turn to find your way spiritually and emotionally? Tim and I have discovered the Bible is an essential road map for life. Reading it on a daily basis provides the best direction we can find. God, who inspired its authors, surpasses all mapmakers. Simply having a Bible for casual reference isn't enough. There's so much to learn and benefit from when you dig deeper.

By day's end, we had wound our way on rural country roads from Moncks Corner to Conway, arriving after eighty-nine miles, just as the maps had directed us. We were in a good, safe place, closer to our destination, and sure to reach it on schedule if we followed the prescribed route—thanks to the guidance and wisdom of others.

The path north along ACA's Atlantic Coast route—the number of roads, choices, and directions to follow—amazed me. It was difficult to see the big picture and the final destination, because the maps are designed in enlarged panels so we can read them while bicycling. Each panel covers only twenty-five to forty miles. To arrive at our destination, we would need to follow one panel at a time—actually, one turn at a time—to avoid getting lost. Others had already figured out the route for us, and we trusted their guidance. Any misstep could foil the directions, and we could find ourselves way off course. Yet, if we followed the directions correctly, we would make it to our goal.

A faith walk with God works in a similar fashion. Just as ACA's stellar maps led us, turn by turn, out of harm's way and enhanced our experience, the Bible can keep us safe spiritually and deliver us to an abundant life. You may have been told to "live one day at a time." When trusting God with the big picture, our job is to follow Him one day and one act of obedience at a time. He explains how to conduct our lives in His road map for life. It's a great way to live.

The Bible contains instructions that can guide you wherever you go in life. Its time-tested life principles make it the ultimate travel guide. It will help you avoid all sorts of pain. I'm going to follow His Word as best I can, one step at a time, so I will never get lost again. Won't you join me?

Miniature horses in South Carolina

Your word is a lamp to my feet and a light to my path.

PSALM 119:105

Personal REFLECTION:

1. When was the last time you read a book that provided guidance for your life just like a map points you in the right direction? How did it help you?

2. If you've tried reading some of the Bible and found it confusing or difficult, you're not alone. Have you considered an easier translation (there are many)? How about joining a group to learn from one another or asking someone who may be more experienced with the Bible to help you understand the more challenging passages?

3. If you've never read the Bible, or it has been a long time since you've cracked it open, give some thought to reading the first chapter in the Gospel of John before you go to sleep tonight. It will only take five minutes. Find it in the table of contents. John is the fourth book in the New Testament, which contains some accounts of Jesus when He lived on Earth. If that intrigues you, consider reading one chapter a night until you finish the book of John. At that rate, you can complete the entire book in just three weeks.

LESSON 6

A Way Out

When you're off course, you need to take great pains
to get back on course or else you will jeopardize the
achievement of your ultimate goal. And, sometimes,
shortcuts will only get you further off course.

BY TIM

Even with a map or a blueprint, we can sometimes lose our way.
We may have an error in our plan that throws us off course, or
we may fail to follow the plan. Never was losing our way more
apparent than on our ride to Dry Ridge, Kentucky, on day eighty-five
of TheHopeLine Tour.

Debbie and I set out in the morning anticipating more hills and
curves. However, we couldn't have imagined what we were about to
encounter. I mentioned to Debbie that I'd been thinking about how we
hadn't had any serious navigational blunders like the ones on our first
cross-country trip. As it turned out, that was a poorly timed comment.

Our turn of events—actually, an ill-timed right turn—occurred
relatively early in the day, at an intersection in Sparta. Had I studied the
map, I would have seen that we should have gone straight to stay on our

route. Instead, I followed a sign that pointed to the right for Dry Ridge and then missed a quick left to stay on Route 467 and return to our route.

Unsuspectingly, we headed south on Route 35. A few miles down the road, perhaps still shaking off morning cobwebs, I noticed we were climbing a long, gradual hill.

"They made another error on these bicycling maps," I said to Debbie. "This hill isn't shown until after Folsom, but they should've shown it here."

In my overconfidence, it never occurred to me that I was the one in error!

A few miles later, it dawned on me that we were cycling with a tail-wind, and that I hadn't seen a sign reading "Route 467" in quite some time. The ones I saw read "Route 35" instead! I also noticed more traffic and better road conditions on that stretch of road than we'd had on Route 467 before Sparta.

I decided to ask for advice from "Garmin," the GPS clipped to my bicycle. Sure enough, we were off course. When I asked the GPS to send me to Dry Ridge, it routed us back toward Route 467, which was to our north.

After some review, I could see that we'd traveled at a 45-degree angle to the correct route. We were headed southeast rather than east. We had a choice to make: reverse direction until we returned to the intersection where we'd taken the wrong turn, or change direction and intercept the correct route farther east. Reversing direction didn't make sense, because we'd be backtracking. And I hate backtracking.

I noticed Route 127 on the map—a major road connecting the road we were on to the one we needed to be on. Garmin's route to Dry Ridge included that road. It seemed reasonable to continue the few miles needed to hit that road and then travel north to our intended route. The error would cost us four or five extra miles, but eventually, we'd be back on course.

Soon, Route 127 appeared, as expected. We turned left and headed north toward Route 467. As we approached it, Garmin offered a shortcut.

I told Debbie, who was riding ahead of me, to follow Garmin's suggestion and turn right. We were so close to the correct route we couldn't get too far off course, or so I thought.

We traveled four miles down a beautiful ridge road. I could see Garmin's mileage to Dry Ridge shrinking with every curve, and there were many. We seemed to be in a good place. Eventually, however, we came to a steep descent—hazardously steep. We braked constantly to control our heavily loaded bicycles down that grade. The road began to narrow and deteriorate as we descended. By the time we dropped to the bottom, the pavement had vanished, replaced by a narrow gravel path with grass growing in the middle.

With my blind faith in Garmin and Debbie's unwavering trust in me, we followed this path until the gravel disappeared—in favor of mud. The road eventually trailed off into high brush and muck. We cycled around several fields looking for an outlet that would allow us to join the traffic we could hear whizzing by on the other side of a stand of trees. I had never imagined our tour would take us onto bumpy farm paths circumventing large tobacco fields. This classic helmet cam footage captured the confusion well, my navigational blunder caught on "film" for the whole world to enjoy:

http://youtu.be/DpWrg2QIcCg

After several foiled attempts to find the secret passage in any direction, we realized we were hemmed in. We were at the bottom of a monster hill with no way out except to reverse direction, get back up the hill somehow, and backtrack to get back on our route. We did just that.

I had compounded my earlier mistake. We pedaled fifteen extra miles and lost two hours searching for a way out. From the sounds of nearby traffic and Garmin's directions, we knew we were so close. Yet a road-block in the form of a river had intervened. Someone told us later (in all seriousness) that the road did indeed connect as Garmin had indicated, but "you needed to cross the 'crick'—and, yes, you would get wet!" An innocent mistake, a lack of focus, and suddenly we were off course.

It's easier than we might think to get off course as we navigate through life. Once we realize we're lost, it's not always clear how to get back on track. In our case, we had to take perhaps the most difficult route, or at least the hardest one to swallow. For, when you reverse direction, you admit to a big mistake. You eat humble pie. It might be good for you, but it never tastes that way!

Other times, we are oh so close to our destination, but people, habits, fears, or circumstances block us. There's always a way out but not always an easy one. Mistakes can be costly. Yet we shouldn't let that keep us from correcting them. Nor should we let them discourage us to the point of simply giving up.

Let your eyes look straight ahead, and your eyelids look right before you. Ponder the path of your feet, and let all your ways be established.

PROVERBS 4:25-26

Personal REFLECTION:

1. When was the last time you took a shortcut and got off track in your personal life?

2. How can you make up the ground you lost when you got off track?

3. What is the best way to avoid shortcuts that lead to problems?

LESSON 7

My Two Dads

Others have already gone before us. You need look no
further than your parents. Appreciate them and their
guidance while you still have them. You can't tell them
you love them once they are gone.

BY DEBBIE

We stayed in Medina, Ohio, for several days in the latter
stages of TheHopeLine Tour to rest and revive ourselves
after ninety-two days on the road. It's easy to remember
the scene, because we were there on some very important dates.

We arrived in Medina on October 2, 2014, which would have
been my dad's eighty-ninth birthday. My sister sent me a text message
with a picture of the two of them at his nursing home in February,
when I visited him for what would be the last time. As I rode my
bike toward Medina, I thought about my dad and the lessons I'd
learned from him over the years.

I pictured him running behind me, holding my bike seat, as I
first pedaled without training wheels. He was there to catch me if
I fell. I also visualized our many times skiing together in New York
and Vermont when I was a young girl.

The end of our trip was approaching, and Tim and I both felt exhausted. I did not want to bicycle on that particular day. However, we rode anyway, because cold weather would be coming in soon, along with rain. My dad's much-needed encouragement came to mind: *"Sometimes, 'Deb Deb,' you have to do things you don't want to do, and that builds character."* I am so grateful for the memories I have of my dad. Honoring him on his birthday made the miles fly by. Thanks, Dad, for teaching me how to ride a bike and holding me up until I could do so on my own.

I had another dad, too. Bill was my stepdad for almost twenty-five years. He and my mom had been planning a trip to New England that September when illness waylaid him before they boarded the plane. For three weeks, he was in the hospital with pneumonia and other health issues. Bill was moved to hospice on my biological dad's birthday, and he passed away there a day later. It was hard to lose two dads in less than a year, but I am blessed with many good memories of the two of them.

I will always remember Bill's kindness and his listening ear. He was so different from my biological dad, quieter and more serious, and I loved them both for their unique traits. When I spent time with Bill and my mom at their Cape Cod home, we would go out for coffee ice cream. He would listen to the latest news about my job, grad school, or whatever I was doing at the time. He was soft-spoken and very smart. I loved him dearly.

Every time I called them, Bill would answer the phone with, "Oh hi, Deb. I'll go get your mom." I'd say, "Wait a minute, Bill, how are *you* doing?" And he would always say "Good," despite his declining health. I will treasure the time I had with him.

Bill's final hospitalization and the uncertainty surrounding it remind me about hope. He was very weak, and family members were wondering whether he would survive. Then, a few good days with a good appetite, more alertness, and improved breathing renewed hope that he would improve and be out of the hospital soon. Yet again, things took a turn for the worse, but he bounced back. When I spoke with my mom, I could hear the hope in her voice. However, at age eighty-seven, it was hard for him to bounce back again.

I knew Bill would have wanted us to finish that tour. So, with no immediate funeral service planned, we would do just that, Lord willing. We would make an additional donation to TheHopeLine to honor his life. And I would think about him often.

With my two dads on my mind as we bicycled through Ohio, we enjoyed another beautiful autumn day, very chilly in the morning, only to clear up and warm up throughout the day. We had the privilege of bicycling through central Ohio's Amish country with few cars on the roads and a sampling of bountiful gardens and horse-drawn buggies along the way. With the many rolling hills, I felt like we were back in the Missouri Ozarks.

Amish buggy in central Ohio

One life lesson kept coming to mind as I reflected on my two dads: express love for your loved ones always. My time with my dad in February had been such a gift, because he passed away a month later. Talking to Bill in September on the phone and telling him that I loved him freed me from regret. I saw a sign on an Ohio church marquee that read: "Tell someone you love them today." That is a good habit to develop each day we are on this beautiful Earth.

If your parents are still with you, give them a chance to make a positive impact on your life. Granted, some parents are not the best, and if you listen to the misguided ones, you are sure to go off course. In those instances, find other mature role models who can forewarn you of life's pitfalls and encourage you as you travel through life. However, for most of us, our parents, though imperfect, are a gift. Heed their wise advice while you still have them. They've gone down some roads you will travel soon—and others you will want to avoid! Above all, appreciate them while they are still here.

> **Honor your father and your mother, that your days may be long upon the land which the Lord your God is giving you.**
> EXODUS 20:12

Personal REFLECTION:

1. Consider asking a parent or respected mentor for his or her advice on how to handle a challenge you are facing.

2. When was the last time you told that parent/mentor you loved him or her? How do you think he or she would react if you did?

3. What would be the best way to express your appreciation to your parent/mentor?

LESSON 8

Fork in the Road

Sometimes, it isn't clear which path to take. Your instincts
and providence can guide you through only after you've
made a decision and begun to move.

BY TIM

On our first trip through Ohio on our honeymoon tour, we
faced a decision about which road to travel out of the east
side of Cleveland. When I asked the desk clerk at the Super 8
in Milan for her advice, she looked alarmed. After she got over her
initial shock, she seemed hesitant to offer an opinion. Perhaps she
was concerned about becoming an accomplice to a crime—not one
we would commit but one that might be perpetrated upon us. Her
reaction gave me the chills. It also validated my own concern about
cycling through a city like Cleveland.

"There are places on the east side of Cleveland that you shouldn't
go!" she said finally. She gave no specifics and no reasons, even when
I pressed her, except for those that I could assume or glean from the
steely look on her grave countenance.

When you come from small-town America, as I do, you're cautious about entering large cities, whether by car or public transportation. The increased activity and the unknown environment induce fear. Entering a large city by bicycle seemed outlandish. Yet our Adventure Cycling Association maps were directing us right through downtown Cleveland. Deviating from maps that had navigated us so skillfully across the better part of America seemed foolish, especially since we were embedded in an urban area without other navigational aids. Bicyclists had followed those maps regularly. We'd have to trust that the routes had been selected for good reasons, with safety in mind.

Yet those same maps were increasing my anxiety by presenting us with a choice of routes. We could take the route along Lake Erie, which seemed flatter and more direct, or we could follow the one through the Highlands section of Cleveland.

We needed some *good* advice. That's what had prompted my query in Milan. The desk clerk's unsettling reaction convinced me we needed more input. Therefore, on our way to the city, I asked the opinion of a local bicyclist whom Debbie and I met at a suburban park.

"Sure, I've heard of horror stories about bicyclists getting attacked on their bikes over there," he said. "But that doesn't stop me from riding there. That's where I've had some of my best rides."

With that "rave endorsement" in hand, Debbie and I took a rest day, which would allow us to consider our urban escape route with clearer heads. What bothered me, however, was that Debbie did not seem very concerned about either route. She wasn't afraid at all. Did she understand that inner cities have gangs? Had she considered she might be a target because she is a woman (and a very good-looking one at that)? Her carefree attitude fueled a discomfort within me that translated into an intense focus on steering us clear of disaster.

We took the bus into downtown Cleveland and visited its lake-front, which nudged my waning confidence. We walked some of the streets and felt safe. Although our bus excursion was about pleasure and relaxation, it was also an opportunity to gather more intelligence about our upcoming ride to more tranquil surroundings somewhere well east of Cleveland.

We decided to take the more direct route through the city. A tight timeline helped seal that decision. We also decided to travel early in the day, when any hoodlums would still be sleeping off the prior night's action. Simply committing to one of the routes provided some comfort, even though we faced an unclear path ahead. Making a decision always delivers comfort, because then we can rely on our faith, which we bring with us to any endeavor. It comes from deep within us. We don't even need to pack it separately.

Ultimately, we cycled through the heart of downtown and out an industrial park on the east side. We met very few people and encountered little activity. Yes, some unwelcome comments came our way, and we saw some angry-looking people, but they minded their own business, as did we.

After our escape, we relaxed and returned to the more carefree attitude we'd come to expect on our tour. We ended the day in Conneaut, Ohio, after ninety-one miles, on the threshold of yet another state. We were right on track. Although we wondered what the other route would have been like, it mattered not. We were in a good place with our eyes looking straight ahead, anticipating new adventures in the coming days. There was no need to look back. Cleveland was already becoming a distant memory.

Often, we face similar crossroads in life. Multiple options will set us on different courses with their own attendant consequences. When in doubt, it helps to seek advice from others who might have traveled down those roads already—and to be discerning about what you hear. Don't allow conflicting advice to stop your progress. Advisors can warn you, allay your fears, and let you know what to expect. Yet you'll never know exactly what you'll encounter until you travel the road yourself. And before you move ahead, you'll never be 100 percent certain which road will bring you to your intended destination. Once you venture forth, you'll be able to adjust your course when needed along the way. When you proceed with confidence, you'll discover your destiny.

· ·

Without counsel, plans go awry, but in the multitude of counselors they are established.

PROVERBS 15:22

· ·

Personal REFLECTION:

1. When seeking advice on a major decision, how do you decide whom to ask?

2. What impending decision is causing you fear and anxiety right now?

3. Think of two people with relevant experience who can advise you on the alternatives. Resolve to speak with at least one of them in the next few days and then move forward with your decision before the end of the week.

LESSON 9

Trading Time

In life, distractions abound. Be prepared to face
some tough decisions on how you will spend your time.
There's always a trade-off!

BY DEBBIE

The Midwest is renowned for the friendliness and hospitality
of its residents. A visit to some farms outside of Wabash,
Indiana, on our first tour confirmed that. Spending much
of an afternoon on a donkey farm and then with a farmer's widow
weren't on my bucket list, but that day will be a treasured memory
for the rest of my life.

I was delighted when I spotted the miniature donkeys, especially
after our harrowing ride the day before on decrepit and congested roads.
When we stopped to admire those cute creations, the man tending the
donkeys invited me over the fence for a close-up view.

As I walked through the herd, I found them docile and friendly.
To my right, a protective mother sheltered her foal from the other
donkeys—and from me. Her shy offspring, the smallest of the small,

wasn't ready for the attention the older foals enjoyed. I don't know how much time passed at the donkey farm, but it was fun petting them. Tim took several photos, but we needed to get moving.

Mothering on display in Indiana

We were anxious to maximize the daylight and arrive home in time for me to start the new school year. Ideally, I wanted to be home in twelve days so I could prepare before students arrived five days thereafter. However, we were nearly one thousand miles away. Time management has always been a weakness of mine. I am distracted easily and think that I can multitask with the best of them, but if I'm completely honest, I can't. I would much rather talk to people than complete a task. And the task we had for that day was to bicycle as many miles as we could.

No sooner had we left the donkey show than another friendly Hoosier called out to us.

"Do you want some lemonade and watermelon?"

A woman was running out toward us as we approached her large farmhouse, her arms flailing in excitement at the sight of travelers in need of hospitality. We stopped and accepted her invitation to escape the heat of the day. How could we turn it down?

The woman and her grandson—one of thirty-four grandchildren, though the only one in attendance at our "party"—delighted us with their company. The young boy strutted around the living room, showcasing his Indiana Pacers jersey while we visited with his grandmother. The ice-cold lemonade and the sweet watermelon cooled me down instantly. Tim and I quickly consumed all of the ice in her ice-cube trays as we listened to their tales of life on the farm. She shared openly about her family and the farm's uncertain future since her husband's passing. I could have spent the entire day and night with that kind, generous woman and her exuberant grandson.

After about an hour, six slices of watermelon, and countless glasses of lemonade, the time came for us to be on our way, all too soon. Riding in the dark is never a good idea, but with all of our delays, we were bound to be using headlamps a few hours later.

What a joy to be invited by a stranger along the road for some refreshment. Would this happen in any other part of the country? Midwestern hospitality in the heart of Indiana made my heart sing.

Choices on how to spend time await everyone. We all have twenty-four hours a day. I prefer to spend my time with people. Others spend their time on tasks or any of a myriad of other choices. Balance is the key. I shouldn't spend all of my time with people, just as a taskmaster shouldn't spend all of his or her time working in isolation. We need to strike a healthy balance between relationships and work.

I hope to improve in my time management, because I can never retrieve the time I've wasted. Building quality relationships leads to an abundant life, so I must make wise decisions about how I spend my time on all of my relationships. Praying about which relationships to pursue and which to let go is essential.

Do you struggle with time management? Distractions come at us with the best of intentions, yet they can leave us off track and behind schedule. You don't want to live life bound to an inflexible plan that squelches the joy of spontaneity. Neither do you want your side trips to prevent you from seizing the best that life has to offer. One thing is certain: you can't do everything you'd like to do, because choosing one activity essentially eliminates another. You're trading one for the other. Make sure you spend your time wisely. There's only so much of it to go around.

> So teach us to number our days, that we may
> gain a heart of wisdom.
>
> PSALM 90:12

Personal REFLECTION:

1. Which people and what activities are most important to you?

2. How much of your discretionary time do you devote to the more important parts of your life?

3. Consider keeping track of how you spend your time for a week. Compare the results to how you think you spend your time and then make any necessary adjustments.

LESSON 10

Fast Fixes Aren't Always the Fastest

You've heard it said, "Haste makes waste." Well, it's true.
Take the time to do things right the first time.

BY TIM

As Debbie and I approached New England on our first tour, we were motivated to cycle as many miles a day as we could. It was bad timing, therefore, when our free breakfast at the motel in Fulton, New York, came with a price: dreadfully slow service. With what we hoped would be a long day in the saddle ahead of us, I wasn't in the mood to tolerate the delay, but we needed ample calories. So despite some heavy toe-tapping, we waited it out. We gulped down the cook's tardy offering thirty minutes later and checked out of the motel.

Late August in upstate New York had brought cooler temperatures. We'd been acclimating after some hot and humid riding a few weeks earlier in the Midwest. Yet this particular morning came with a biting wind that penetrated our scant layers even before we mounted our saddles. We weren't bashful about taking more time to dive back into our bags for warmer clothing despite our late start.

If you're far enough upstate in New York, you're bound to see some big, billowy clouds rolling off Lake Ontario. We were close to the lake, so close we had touched it at Sodus Point on the prior day. We had seen massive clouds. Some were white, but most were predominantly dark, storing up a downpour for just the right (or wrong) moment. Soon, we'd see some more big black ones.

We cycled north and east toward the lake again. The sight of water provided some relief from the rural panorama. The lakeside riding came with more activity and fewer trees and hills. Then, finally, after thirty-odd miles, we came to the town of Pulaski.

As we headed into town, I commented to Debbie, "My rear tire doesn't feel right. It's squishy."

Several hundred feet later, another downward glance revealed why. My rear tire was going flat. *Oh, great,* I thought. *Just what we need to slow our progress even more.* With only one flat tire in three thousand miles, we had forgotten that tubes do indeed fail. I slowed to a stop and located a mailbox that would serve as a useful prop for the bicycle as I began the repair.

Rear-tire tubes are more difficult to repair or replace than front ones, because the chain must be removed from the rear cassette and derailleur cogs and then put back the right way. It's not a big deal for most bicycle tourists to change a rear tire. However, Debbie and I aren't your typical tourists. We're mechanically challenged. I'd replaced quite a few tubes on my road bike, and my touring bicycle was similar. So, I knew I could figure out how to fix it. I just wanted to finish the job and get back on the road as soon as possible. We were already behind schedule, and now we were losing more valuable time.

I wrestled with the heavy, bulky bicycle and then decided to remove the panniers, because I couldn't balance the bicycle and work on it. Meanwhile, Debbie located the tools and handed them to me. A young man who had heard our commotion from an open window emerged from the house on the corner as I removed the rear tire.

"Do you need any tools or any help?" he offered. He was wearing a T-shirt with a logo for a Christian school, which I found reassuring, since I'd volunteered for years helping a Christian school with their accounting. Nevertheless, I thought I could handle the repair more quickly with just the two of us. I thanked him but declined his offer.

Eventually, I removed the tire and replaced the tube. I pumped the tire up enough to see if it would hold air, and then I installed it onto the bicycle and blew it up to capacity. Soon, we were off toward the center of town. We had only lost about a half hour on the repair job, so I felt affirmed in my attempt to keep us rolling. Meanwhile, the heavy cloud cover darkened.

When we arrived in town, we pulled up to a convenience store for a break. It was a timely stop. When I looked down at the newly repaired tire, it was flat…again. Maybe the young man at our last stop would have performed the repair more proficiently than I had.

While Debbie was inside, I repaired the tire again, faster this time thanks to my "practice attempt" a few minutes earlier. In my haste the first time, I had failed to diagnose the cause of the flat. Sure enough, as my hand swathed the inside of the tire, I felt a tiny wire protruding from the tread, which no doubt had caused the two flats. I removed the wire, replaced the tube, and mounted the tire. Then we departed.

We were cycling deeper into the woods before long. Perhaps I had become paranoid, but the ride seemed very bumpy. The rear wheel still did not feel right. I got off and tested the rear wheel for wobble. It looked fine. Suspecting the tube had not fully unfurled, I removed some air and re-inflated the tire. Finally, the problem seemed to be behind us. The storm clouds, however, were not.

They had vaulted on ahead without us. Although I regretted losing valuable time due to my negligence and hastiness on the first repair job, that cloud had a silver lining. Soon, we were cycling through large puddles in the road. We had avoided a downpour.

Sometimes, we travel through life too fast. We end up costing ourselves more time than if we had thought things through in the first place. It's comforting when God overlooks our recklessness and coordinates the random forces of nature with our own fumbling to bring about special blessings—or to prevent nasty outcomes. It's just one benefit we encounter when we surrender to His providence.

- -

He has not dealt with us according to our sins,
nor punished us according to our iniquities.
PSALM 103:10

- -

Personal REFLECTION:

1. Do you find yourself having to repeat chores because you hurried through them the first time?

2. Do you have an unfinished task that someone who is more adept can help you with or teach you how to accomplish more efficiently?

3. Think about the last task you rushed through but weren't satisfied with the results. How might you have done it differently?

SECTION

II

Shifting Gears

You set out on your own unique journey anticipating adventure. Your accelerating heartbeat confirms your decision to embark on something truly life changing. The exhilaration of the open road, the wind against your face, and the breathtaking scenery of your new surroundings captivate you. However, no plans are foolproof. You'll need to make some adjustments along the way.

Change will happen on any successful trip. If you're unwilling to adapt, your destination will merely remain an unachieved goal. Embracing change makes the intended outcome of any endeavor feasible and draws it into clearer focus. So, revise your plans as necessary, and hang on for the ride. You'll be there before you know it!

SECTION II TAKEAWAYS

Things to Adjust

1.

2.

3.

4.

5.

LESSON 11

Change Is Inevitable

Opportunities can drift by, leaving those who refuse to change in their wake. Choosing to collaborate with change rather than compete with it will bring opportunity—and better headway on your trip—well within your grasp.

BY TIM

After the challenges of negotiating roadways designed for motorized vehicles for days on end, a wonderful, leisurely ride alongside the Erie Canal provided welcome relief on our honeymoon tour. No noise, no nasty smells, no traffic, no hills, no people. Just birds chirping amid the lush greenery of New York State, which surrounded the placid waters on a pleasant, sunshiny day in late August.

Those in charge in New York have done a commendable job adapting a transportation marvel of yesteryear to a quaint, alternative use as it nears the end of its life cycle. I first learned about the Erie Canal umpteen years ago in school. On day fifty-three of our honeymoon tour, I learned about it firsthand from the seat of a bicycle. Modern placards, which documented timelines and once-revolutionary ways of doing business, lined the canal while its passersby could only speculate on the billions of dollars of cargo that had floated down its humble waters. Debbie and I enjoyed our ride through history and the benefits for those who chose to reflect on that passageway's significance in growing North American businesses.

Erie Canal tugboat

It must have been a tremendous effort to dredge a long canal in the 1820s and to expand it one hundred years later. According to http://eriecanal.org, the canal took seven years to build, and without the aid of any of today's mechanization. The same website quotes the key statistics of the earlier design as follows:

- 363 miles in length
- 40 feet wide
- 4 feet deep
- 75 tons of maximum displacement
- 77 locks

The Erie Canal played an extraordinary role in our nation's history and in its industrial revolution. However, what we saw hardly looked industrial—or revolutionary. We'd never seen such archaic-looking vessels as we witnessed on our ride from Medina to Pittsford, New York. We were cycling through a marine museum cast in its original setting.

What we experienced was a peaceful ride on crushed gravel along a ditch filled with stagnant, murky water. I could have tossed a rock to the other side of the narrow channel with little effort. *Big commerce traveled through here?* It was hard to believe. Not even the sharp blue and yellow paint jobs that adorned the ancient tugs, barges, and equipment could convince me. Try as the authorities might, I couldn't help but wonder when the cost of prolonging the canal's life would bring about an inevitable change.

In Cleveland, we had seen a large ship docked on the shore of Lake Erie. My imagination could not fathom that ship fitting in the narrow, shallow channel beside which we cycled. The canal has become a relic of a bygone era. Facelifts and paint jobs notwithstanding, it is entertaining cyclists along its flat towpaths or those who wish to travel its unique and tranquil passageways via pleasure craft. Leisure was nowhere in sight in the early 1800s when the canal was merely a gleam in engineers' eyes, yet man's creativity and our resistance to letting go of the past have adapted this outdated artifact to squeeze every last cent out of it before we all say our good-byes for good.

The more we traveled and the more we read, the more I could envision backroom political discussions on how—and whether—to perpetuate what no longer fit and was costly to maintain. Yet the emotional cost of surrendering what once treated us well makes letting go feel sacrilegious. The temptation is to hold on to the past, but the longer we hold on, the more costly it becomes.

When an institution of such historical significance as the Erie Canal becomes obsolete, saying good-bye can be difficult. But with time and human ingenuity, more efficient and cost-effective techniques arise. If you live in the past long enough, you'll be abandoned to what once was but no longer should be.

We have similar edifices in our own lives. To remove or change them can be emotionally painful and may involve swallowing some pride. But to limp along year after year only allows more blood in the bandage and prevents new growth from taking root. Refusing to change will cost you time, money, and opportunity.

Do you have some "modernization programs" screaming for your attention? Are you still doing things the old-fashioned way? Do you refuse to learn and participate in new ways of communicating? A thoughtful and thorough self-examination will take into account the cost of maintaining the status quo. You may be paying good money, time, or attention to sustain what no longer keeps pace while the world passes you by. That's just too high a price.

· ·

**To everything there is a season, a time
for every purpose under heaven.**
ECCLESIASTES 3:1

· ·

Personal REFLECTION:

1. Has someone younger than you been trying to get you to try something new recently? What is holding you back?

2. When you think about some people you know in your parents' generation, do they resist change or do they accept it readily? What about people in your generation?

3. Have you seen some new technology that could make your life easier or more fulfilling by freeing up some of your time? Consider trying it out.

LESSON 12

Growing Means Changing

To grow, one must let go of certain things from the past.
Although this change may be difficult, that doesn't mean
it can't or shouldn't happen.

BY DEBBIE

If you'd like to get to know someone really well, consider taking a long-distance bicycle tour with that person! You'll get to know your travel partner quickly. You can learn about the person through daily life, but it might take you twice as long compared to an intense bicycle tour together. While cycling from Oregon to Maine on our honeymoon tour, Tim and I were in close quarters for almost two months. I learned plenty during that time, and not just about the beautiful land that surrounded us.

God seems to put people together who are quite different from one another. Tim and I have many interests in common, but our backgrounds and personalities could not be more different. Furthermore, we had things our own way for many years as singles. Those factors made for some head-butting but also some interesting adjustments and personal revelations as we cycled east. Thank goodness we weren't on a tandem bicycle!

In Oregon and Washington, we had some intense conflict stemming from our different approaches to life. Tim usually calculates his decisions, and I tend to make mine spontaneously. He also exercises more caution than I do. Given our differences, I wanted to experience adventure more than he did. I wanted to make the most of our journey into the unknown. He was more concerned about navigation and safety.

As we continued farther east, we came to realize that we needed to allow for each other's differences. We couldn't simply do things our own way, even though both of us were accustomed to that approach from our single lives. Cycling with another person means you must share a common agenda. You need each other and must stay united. Tim and I had chosen a self-supported tour. If we didn't stick together, we wouldn't be able to help one another. Therefore, we had to compromise. I didn't realize how selfish I had become as a single person.

Two are better.

Making decisions together as we pedaled across America on our honeymoon became easier by the time we hit New York. We needed each other's cooperation to keep moving forward. Coming home and returning to stress at work, a different type of close quarters, and mundane, daily tasks would be more challenging than being on the open road together. I discovered that I needed to change my perspective and surrender my single lifestyle to be happily married.

Tim and I also have different spiritual backgrounds, although we've landed on common ground. He became a Christian at age eight, twenty-three years before I did. Having that firm foundation has provided him with the ability to face life head-on with strength and assurance. My gift of desperation for God's deliverance came when I realized I could not continue destroying my life. My eating disorder and alcoholism had distanced me from the people I loved, and had damaged family relationships and friendships. Asking Jesus into my life at age thirty-one reversed that trend and began a discovery process that will continue for the rest of my life.

When I grew up, we did not talk much about God in our home, so I began to learn about faith on my own as an adult. Today, I love reading the Bible, writing to the Lord in my journal, and memorizing Scripture. I joined Alcoholics Anonymous at the same time I became a Christian. The Lord has taught me many things through recovery meetings, through His Word (the Bible), and through fellow believers at church.

God has been a patient and persistent teacher, my best instructor, in the past quarter century. He has freed me from my addictions as I've trusted in Him. Until I realized how much Jesus loves me, I wasn't capable of truly loving—and being loved by—my husband. As my AA sponsor always said, "We are constantly in the process of becoming." That has been true of my own personal growth, my relationships with others, and my relationship to my Creator.

The description of a wife of noble character in Proverbs 31 was an excellent starting point for me to learn how to be the kind of married woman God wants me to be. Some of the outstanding questions I've asked myself include: *Does my husband have full confidence in me?* (v. 11), *Do I bring him good and not harm all the days of my life?* (v. 12), *Do I set about my work vigorously?* (v. 17), *Do I open my arms to the poor and extend my hands to the needy?* (v. 20), and *Am I clothed with strength and dignity, and do I speak with wisdom?* (vv. 25-26).

Being single for fifty-two years carved into my being self-sufficiency, independence, and self-centeredness. Those qualities don't enhance married life. I've had to surrender my life as a single and ask God to help me become the wife my husband needs. Similarly, Tim will tell you that he needs to love me sacrificially, just as Christ laid down His life for the people He loves—each and every one of us.

Being open to transformation releases unlimited potential to grow in every aspect of life. I need God's help to show me what areas of my life to give up, to change, and to learn anew, especially as a married person. When two lives merge, friction is inevitable, particularly after living solo for several decades. Starting our marriage with a long bicycle trip was a beautiful bonding experience. We learned that we have to keep pedaling to finish the ride regardless of the trouble or conflict we experience. I've come to appreciate the benefits of Tim's cautious approach to bicycle travel. He loves me and wants me to be safe. Likewise, my love of adventure has motivated Tim to enjoy more of life.

Marriage, of course, involves much more than simply pedaling and seeing some beautiful scenery. It entails ridding yourself of selfishness, sacrificing for your spouse, and living in the order of JOY (Jesus, Others, Yourself). I think I'll adopt this motto: "If I put myself last, my marriage will last!" If all couples took this approach, wouldn't that make a big difference in marriages today? I don't know the statistics, but selfishness has to be the number one cause of divorce. Yet who wants to admit to being selfish?

What do you need to change? If you're married, God can help you see your blind spots and change what needs changing. All you have to do is ask for His help. After all, if you believe what the Bible says, He's the One who united you to your spouse at the altar, and He knows both of you better than anyone else does. Won't you ask for some guidance today for the sake of the best marriage possible? Benefits await you for many years to come!

> **Whoever seeks to save his life will lose it,**
> **and whoever loses his life will preserve it.**
>
> LUKE 17:33

Personal REFLECTION:

1. When you consider the prospect of change in your life, what aspect of that change brings either comfort or discomfort? Why?

2. Many experts characterize personal growth as a lifelong process rather than the attainment of a certain age or status. How might a process view of growth benefit you?

3. Are you feeling some pressure to change something about yourself or your circumstances? What's preventing you from moving forward?

LESSON 13

Two Attached and Too Attached

*Becoming too attached can throw you out of kilter
when what you are attached to goes away.*

BY DEBBIE

As I held my Keen sandal over the garbage can in the motel room in Rugby, North Dakota, I couldn't believe what I was about to do. But at least I was no longer crying about it. An unfortunate event on the road that day had taught me an important lesson I thought I already knew. When we embarked on our honeymoon tour across the country weeks earlier, I was shocked and elated at the joy of minimizing my belongings for two months on the road. Then, "the sandal incident" happened.

It started early in the day. Usually, Tim and I packed everything into our panniers before we headed out each morning. I would attach the damp laundry that I washed out the night before to let the clothes dry in the wind as we biked throughout the day. I would also weave bike shorts and tops through the straps on my panniers, and bungee cord the socks and other items to my back rack.

Only the bare necessities

When we headed out of Minot, North Dakota, that morning, I decided to bungee cord my Keen sandals to my rear rack to freshen them up in the sun and wind. I should note that Keen sandals are among my absolute favorite possessions. Not only are they comfortable and supportive, I can also slip them on and off easily. When they get wet, they dry quickly. I can walk through puddles, into the ocean, and up mountains with those sandals. Although more expensive and a bit heavier than the alternatives, they are the perfect shoe for a warm-weather bicycle tour.

The traffic was horrific on US Route 2 in Towner despite the divided highway. The roadway was under construction, which made it abnormally narrow. We had to stay alert. To our left, speedy traffic crowded us.

Meanwhile, we tried to stay on the narrow shoulder without riding onto the rumble strip, which would jar our bodies and our bicycles. Tim and I always tried to stay within sight of each other, but as we concentrated on our steering, he slipped out of sight ahead of me.

Soon, amid the noise of passing traffic, I heard a foreign sound emanating from the back of my bike. I am not proud of the fact that I tend to ignore noises that indicate a possible malfunction, either on my bicycle or in my car. Disregarding these warnings is neither safe nor wise, especially on a long-distance bicycle tour. After all, I needed the bike to get home. A week earlier in Montana, I had continued riding while my loose back rack came crashing to the ground, panniers and all. My left pannier still bore a scar, patched with duct tape. So, I stopped reluctantly to check out the clanking sound.

I discovered a bungee cord had come loose, and its metal hook was dangling against the spokes on my back wheel. Thankfully, it had not yet caught onto any of the spokes and damaged them. As I looked closer, I saw only one Keen sandal strapped to the other bungee cord. A sick feeling washed over me. *Where's my other sandal?* A scan of my immediate surroundings revealed no sign of it.

Riding back to find my beloved sandal seemed like a bad idea. I had no idea where it had fallen off. The perilously narrow shoulder on a road reduced to only one lane made it clear I shouldn't turn around and head back into traffic. Furthermore, Tim was nowhere in sight. I could no longer hold back the tears.

As I fixed the loose bungee cord and double-checked to see that my spokes were intact, my phone rang. It was Tim.

"Where are you?" he asked.

My sniffles must have alarmed him, because, after a pause, I heard him say, "Are you okay?"

He had waited for me up ahead for several minutes and was concerned about what might have happened to me. He was grateful that I was okay and the bike was not damaged, but he did not comprehend my sadness over my lost sandal. Not only would I not find a pair of Keen sandals in this part of the country, where work boots were the norm, I would not feel comfortable spending another ninety dollars on a pair of sandals while on a pricey bicycle tour. Since we were only halfway through our trip, I'd need to replace them with a cheaper pair of footwear at Walmart.

I am a bit embarrassed to say I felt heartbroken. Never had I spent that much money on a pair of sandals, which I thought would last me a lifetime. To lose only one merely added to the anguish. What good would only one sandal do? I couldn't buy another one for forty-five dollars to salvage the pair. I had enough weight on my bicycle already, so I chose to get over the tears and discard the remaining sandal. My broken heart would mend soon enough.

I didn't realize how attached I had become to the sandals until I lost one. It was just a shoe. My grief was way out of proportion to my loss. What mattered most was that I'd not been harmed and my bicycle hadn't been damaged. We could continue on without a problem.

That incident in North Dakota reminded me once again not to become chained to earthly possessions. One of the beauties of a bicycle tour is minimizing our attachment to things so we can focus on the splendor of what we experience each day. Being too attached to things can weigh us down, whether we're on a long-distance bicycle tour or simply traveling through life.

Material possessions are wonderful to have and convenient for living, but when we become emotionally attached to them, they've become too important to us. Focusing on them can compromise our relationships, and losing them can throw us out of balance.

Similarly, we can become too attached to the people in our lives for all the wrong reasons. When our sense of self-worth depends upon a relationship with someone else—even if that person is our spouse— we can lose our balance when he or she is removed from our life. An unhealthy dependence can also stress the relationship when the person is with us. The only attachment that will not fail us is our connection to our Maker. When you're attached appropriately to the right things, you'll find the freedom to enjoy the splendor that surrounds you each day as you journey through life.

....

If I have made gold my hope, or said to fine gold, "You are my confidence"; this also would be an iniquity deserving of judgment, for I would have denied God who is above.

JOB 31:24, 28

....

Personal REFLECTION:

1. When was the last time you lost something you relished? How did you move on from the loss, and what did you learn from it?

2. Think of your most prized possession. What would you do if it disappeared? Do you think your attachment to it is healthy?

3. Think of one of your relationships in which dependence is lopsided, whether you depend too much upon the other person or vice versa. What adjustments can each of you make to bring about more balance and a healthier relationship going forward?

LESSON 14

Excess Baggage

When your burden is too heavy, you'll bog down. Lightening the load will make for easier and more delightful travel.

BY TIM

On day one of our honeymoon on wheels, we were shaky—very shaky. It was difficult to balance our fully loaded bicycles. You might think that anyone who undertakes a challenge as ambitious as a self-supported, cross-country bicycle tour would be better prepared. Sure, we had ridden our bicycles...a few times. We even rode them loaded with gear. However, we had never loaded them with as much weight as we had at the start of our tour. After all, we'd had a wedding to plan and attend. We had no idea how much food and equipment we would end up with—until we embarked.

So, on the second day of our tour, we relearned how difficult it could be to balance a fully loaded bicycle, and we learned a little more, thanks to the challenging terrain. We discovered that negotiating corners with these oversized rigs was harder than we thought. Loaded touring bikes are bigger and more awkward than regular bicycles. We couldn't simply do a U-turn in the middle of the road to reverse direction.

We were cycling up a long grade on US Route 30, heading east toward Portland, Oregon, when we took a break. We exited the road at a 45-degree angle onto a dirt lane. After our break, turning the bicycles around and starting up the steep hill was challenging, especially with steady traffic and little proven skill to balance our loads at low speeds. We wobbled and weaved as we struggled to control the heavy bicycles. The difficult conditions reminded us of the apprenticeship we had taken only the day before.

US Route 30 along the Columbia River in Oregon

How did we get into this predicament? We had gone to the grocery store with Debbie's cousin Jim. No, I'm not passing the blame. This was our issue, not Jim's. But Jim knows nutrition. Following his advice, we stocked up on healthy snacks. Instead of buying the premixed bag of trail mix, though, we decided to make our own. After all, we'd be consuming plenty of trail mix for energy on our trip. We couldn't be left without food for the energy we'd need later, with no stores for miles. Why pay more for a premixed bag? By making our own mix, we could also decide what to put in it, both the type of food and its quality. (Rationalizing away poor judgment is an unworthy pastime, but I indulge in it from time to time.)

Therefore, we purchased a bag of walnuts, a bag of almonds, a bag of sunflower seeds, a large bag of raisins, a bag of dried fruit, etc. We ended up with a very large bag of trail mix, exactly the way we wanted it. And, boy, was it good!

We wouldn't need that much mix, however, at least not right then. And it was heavy. We'd be eating "healthy" doses of trail mix for days just to lighten the load. We also wondered what other gear was extraneous. We might use some of those items once or twice during our tour, but would they really be necessary?

Have you ever found yourself walking through life with excess baggage? Suddenly, you noticed an extra burden to carry and to manage. Maybe you have one now. You may not know how it became so heavy and unnecessary, or even how it came to be, but you've come to realize you're overloaded. If so, it's time to figure out how to reduce your load so it doesn't bog you down and clutter your life.

Some burdens are easier to discard than others. If you own too much stuff, then organizing and eliminating some of it can be relatively easy once you commit to doing it. The worst kind of clutter is not stuff but hang-ups and emotional baggage. Some people hold on to past hurts and injustices—and the anger, resentment, jealousy, grudges, and bitterness that come with them—for years. Others bog down with unhealthy ways of thinking.

Emotional and behavioral baggage will hold you back more than mere stuff will. Yet it can be more difficult to identify and relinquish. You might need a third party to help you, such as a counselor, pastor, friend, or parent. Although purging this type of baggage can be painful, you'll not regret the cost later when you are free to live a more joyful life and make better progress toward long-held dreams.

Is it time to clean out the closets? More importantly, do you need to forgive someone? Do you need to grieve a loss? Is it time to deal with those inescapable feelings of jealousy that bind you? Maybe it's time to "hang up on the hang-up" or to surrender control of what you can't really control anyway. Choose to unload what keeps you from a more meaningful and fulfilling life. Take the first step today.

For we brought nothing into this world, and it is certain we can carry nothing out. And having food and clothing, with these we shall be content.

1 TIMOTHY 6:7-8

Personal REFLECTION:

1. How much of your time do you spend managing clutter in your life? Do you own some things you haven't used or looked at in the past five years? Who else could use or enjoy them?

2. What bogs you down in your relationships? Has someone wronged you and you're unwilling to let go of the offense? Is something gnawing at you, but you can't put your finger on it? Can someone in your life help you identify the problem?

3. Have you suffered a loss you're still mourning—or need to begin mourning? How can you begin to release this baggage?

LESSON 15

Challenges

One way to guarantee change is to take on a challenge
and resolve to pursue it with reckless abandon.
The greater the challenge, the more likely change
will transform you.

BY DEBBIE

Challenges. We can't live without them, but many times, we don't make an effort to take them on. We take the easier, softer way. When was the last time you really tested yourself? A challenge can take many forms. For example, it could be social, intellectual, physical, or financial. Are you up for a challenge?

When we embarked on TheHopeLine Tour, we thought we were up for a challenge, even though we had no guarantee of success. By its very nature, bicycle touring promises a challenge. If we wanted to get back to Massachusetts, we had a lot of work ahead of us, including over four thousand miles of pedal pushing and who knew how many feet of elevation.

As part of a bigger challenge, each day presented its own unique tests. On day eight, we had our greatest test of the trip to date. I was apprehensive, since it was only our fifth day of riding after a three-day layover outside of Eugene, Oregon, where I'd had a cortisone shot in my knee. Furthermore, the map forecasted a four-thousand-foot climb up to McKenzie Pass. Like most challenges, though, the anticipation was worse than the event. And I must say that event was breathtaking… in a positive way.

We saw an amazing combination of forests, lava fields, and snow-capped mountains. At the foot of the climb, a sign stating that bicycles could use the whole lane added much-needed grace, given the steep drop-offs with no guardrails to separate us from disaster. Traffic was minimal as we climbed the gradual ascents. Later in the day, we cycled on perfect roads with wide shoulders. We averaged only 9.4 miles per hour due to our twenty-two-mile uphill climb, but the challenge was worth it. The satisfaction at the end of the day was priceless.

Satisfaction atop McKenzie Pass in Oregon

As with anyone's walk through life, every state on any route we could have taken would have challenged us. We avoided Colorado's eleven-thousand-foot Hoosier Pass only to face higher heights than we'd ever climbed before elsewhere. No services in Wyoming tested these two inexperienced campers. Skirting Yellowstone, with its grizzly bears and traffic, meant venturing out onto I-90 more than once—at our own peril. We were grateful to miss tornadoes in Kansas, but the heat and humidity caught up with us on a sweltering afternoon in Nebraska. And although Kentucky's wild dogs left us alone, its hills ganged up on us instead. Other challenges we couldn't imagine awaited us. Yet learning to take one day at a time and enjoying one moment at a time kept us focused on the challenge before us and loving the ride along the way.

Raising $100,000 for TheHopeLine seemed like the steepest road ahead. We were feeling blessed to be part of something so... well...*challenging,* yet we knew we didn't have the power to accomplish that feat by ourselves. We could articulate the opportunity and explain the mission, which we did on a webpage entitled "Why Support TheHopeLine?" (http://www.openroadpress.com/links/ thehopeline-tour-2014/why-support-thehopeline/). Yet, ultimately, reaching that goal would depend upon the participation of others. Teenagers and young adults growing up in this world face many challenges. Supporting TheHopeLine helps them climb their mountains and navigate their way through life. Just as we would need help, many of them will need help with their journeys too.

Challenges can be more than merely engaging and invigorating. They can help you focus your way to a better life. They can also be truly life changing. We've found that our touring challenges have helped broaden our perspective, build our confidence, and shape us as individuals and as a couple. We wouldn't trade them for anything. They've allowed us to stretch ourselves in unexpected ways.

We all confront challenges in life, whether or not we choose them. You'll find that tackling the ones that will improve your place in this world will help prevent you from facing challenges not of your own choosing, which are often more difficult to conquer. Doesn't it make sense to chart your own course so it isn't decided for you? You'll receive a higher level of satisfaction and develop a greater ability to meet life head-on when you conquer your most cherished challenges. What would you like to take on today?

For with God nothing will be impossible.

LUKE 1:37

Personal REFLECTION:

1. What scares you more: failure or success? Consider talking to someone about your fear so you can begin to overcome it.

2. What things would you like to change in your life, but you're not sure how to start? What activity have you wanted to accomplish, but its size has intimidated you?

3. Make a commitment to tackle one item you identified from the previous question and ask someone to help hold you accountable. Once you make this commitment and begin to ask questions of others, you'll gain the knowledge and the confidence you need to proceed.

LESSON 16

Remembering the Past

When change is so significant that it transforms
you, you've just been liberated!

BY DEBBIE

It was hard to believe I was a newlywed on a cross-country bicycle
tour, cycling through Pittsford, New York. I graduated from
Sutherland High School there in 1975. Our maps took us along
the Erie Canal, right through town!

Tim and I took a detour and rode our bikes up Winding Road to
the secluded entrance to the home where I had lived from 1969-1975.
Those were difficult years. In the eighth grade, I was introduced to Jesus,
but I instead chose to go my own destructive way. Many memories of my
poor choices flooded back as we rode our bikes through my hometown.

As a young teen, I became anorexic and bulimic. I smoked pot and
started drinking while in middle school. I hungered so much for love
that I kept no boundaries with boys. I was searching for meaning in
my life, yet I had none.

At the same time, my mom and dad were having their own difficulties. They had some intense conflicts, including some while they were drinking. The domestic chaos terrified me.

I became obsessed with exercising and counting calories, which eventually led me to lose fifty-four pounds. I started out as a normal, 135-pound young woman at 5'6" and whittled myself down to a skeletal eighty-one pounds. My parents did not seem to notice my weight loss. Mom's best friend finally pointed out that I might have had anorexia, a condition that has received much more publicity today than it did back then.

Eventually, my eating disorders and my drinking became addictions that controlled my behavior well into my twenties. They wreaked havoc with my relationships and my coping skills. I suffered with the consequences for eighteen difficult years.

The winding road leads home.

Today, I'm in a much better state than when I lived in Pittsford so many years ago, for which I'm so grateful. At the age of thirty-one, my life changed for the better. God's Spirit had been wooing me the whole time, but I didn't ask Him to come into my life until fourteen years after high school.

Remembering where I came from and sharing it with Tim caused me to explode with appreciation. Touching down there again after so many years also caused me to consider "if only." If only I had accepted Jesus into my life in the eighth grade instead of eighteen years later, I could have avoided so much self-inflicted pain. Even so, Jesus didn't waste anything. It's awesome how He redeemed the mistakes in my life. Those tumultuous years of living my way, and the consequences I bore as a result, gave me a gratitude I will always feel. His transforming power is nothing to scoff at. I am truly a new creation. I've been set free from my sin and my past. Our "chance" travel through my hometown served as a helpful reminder of just how far I have come.

As you travel through life, are you reminded of times that you'd just as soon forget? If you've already been set free from your past, let those reminders be opportunities to thank the One who delivered you. If you still struggle with people or behaviors that hold you captive, I hope my story inspires you to believe you don't have to remain a prisoner. Your freedom is only a prayer away. Once you begin to travel the road God has set out for you, you'll receive a peace that surpasses all understanding. And you'll avoid plenty of heartache. You may still encounter some bumps in the road, but you'll never lack for guidance and assurance.

Therefore, if anyone is in Christ, he is a new creation; old things have passed away; behold, all things have become new.

2 CORINTHIANS 5:17

Personal REFLECTION:

1. Have you ever made decisions that caused plenty of heartache? Which of those decisions are still holding you captive?

2. What would transformational change look like in your life now? Are you seeking it? If not, why?

3. Do you think transformational change is possible? How might it take place?

SECTION
III

Taking Precautions

When we're bicycle touring, we undertake some important safety measures. For example, we wear helmets. We're not planning to need them, but the potential costs of not using them—concussions and permanent brain damage—are not worth leaving them behind. We also use rearview mirrors, not to look behind us constantly but to detect upcoming vehicles that might rattle us or strike us.

On your pursuits, the rules you play by and the boundaries you set for yourself will establish many of your precautions. Since everyone has limitations, you'll want to focus your efforts and resources toward what can deliver you to your destination.

Things to Protect Me and Help Focus My Efforts

1. _____

_____

_____

2. _____

_____

_____

3. _____

_____

_____

4. _____

_____

_____

5. _____

_____

_____

LESSON 17

What Do You Value Most?

What you value most will either advance you toward your
goals or prevent you from attaining them. The wrong
values and priorities can derail your trek.

BY TIM

The only thing that separates towns along the Hi-Line, US
Route 2, in eastern Montana is miles and miles of un-
impeded high plains—nothing but grass and wheat, a long
strip of asphalt, and a parallel rail line. The plains are utterly glorious
in their expansiveness. You can see forever and then some.

The suggestive freedom on that open road was contradicted only
by the human strife that seemed to pervade the area. We'd traveled
the Hi-Line for four days on our honeymoon tour. Conversations
with locals spotlighted an irony I found difficult to fathom given the
magnificence of the surrounding landscape. Some of the people there,
we were warned, didn't get along and could be unruly. The locals
strongly urged us to make a beeline for North Dakota.

The Hi-Line in eastern Montana

When you're fifty miles from the next town in a place like that, you feel a bit more vulnerable to equipment failure, to an urgent need for personal services like food or a bathroom, or to people wondering what you are doing on their home turf. So when the bite valve to Debbie's water supply flew off and, abetted by a strong wind, vanished into the tall grass alongside the road, we felt compelled to find it.

Debbie's water began spilling out all over her. On hot days like that one, and especially with long distances between services, we had to preserve as much water as possible. Without the bite valve, a wad of bubble gum might have helped—if we'd had some. Duct tape might have worked in a pinch too, just as it does for about anything else.

Regardless, we didn't have any spare bite valves on board, and, without one, Debbie wouldn't be able to drink frequently enough to endure the heat of the day, let alone those that would follow. We couldn't purchase a specialty part like that at the local convenience store, which was at least thirty miles away.

As Debbie held the gravity-fed hose upright to prevent further loss of water, we looked for the missing part, carefully reconstructing the incident to narrow down our search. A half hour later, we had exhausted our efforts with nothing to show for them. An eighty-mile day awaited us. Any more time spent searching would probably be unfruitful and would only cost us more time. We needed to make special provisions for Debbie's water supply.

Something of such little monetary value can become priceless to the right person under the right circumstances. We often take things for granted until circumstances change. Suddenly, the seemingly insignificant becomes the lynchpin to bailing us out of a dilemma—or to fulfilling our mission. Debbie and I didn't appreciate a bite valve until we discovered the hard way that we couldn't get along without it.

It certainly is curious how we ascribe value to things. If we keep coming back to the monetary measure, we'll be disappointed. That scale doesn't always work. An old photograph of a lost love, a timely piece of advice from a mentor, a meaningful relationship with a trusted friend, or a difficult life lesson learned years ago in the school of hard knocks are treasures of infinite value that money can't buy. You won't find inspiration or wisdom on sale at the local department store...or at a high-end auction house. You may not even find them at institutions of higher learning.

What do you need to pursue your goals and dreams? I guarantee you it's not just money or possessions. If you focus too much on acquiring such things and then assume the burden of managing them, you may never find your way out of the wilderness. You'll be too busy or just plain distracted.

As for us, our roadside quandary ended well. As we began to cycle away from the scene, Debbie's last glance toward the side of the road spotted the bite valve, propped up in a tuft of tall grass. Wow! Heaven had just returned our phone call.

· ·

For where your treasure is, there your heart will be also.

MATTHEW 6:21

· ·

Personal REFLECTION:

1. If your house was on fire and you had time to retrieve only three things before escaping with your life, what would they be?

2. If your doctor said you had only three months to live, how would you spend your remaining time?

3. When you arrive at the end of your life, what legacy would you like to leave behind?

LESSON 18

Hanging on Too Tightly

Hanging on too tightly can squeeze the life out of anything. Letting go, on the other hand, can be liberating.

BY TIM

After several days cranking out long mileage in 90-degree heat on the Mom-to-Mom Tour, one particular morning came too early—thanks in part to some noisy neighbors. Some extra shuteye to compensate resulted in a nine o'clock departure, with the sun already amped up to challenge our progress. Our late start and the cumulative effect of pushing ourselves to the limit took their toll, but we still managed fifty-four miles by day's end.

That day introduced us to North Carolina. We zigzagged north and east to US Route 17 and then crossed the border from South Carolina on Route 179. Brisk traffic in both states, particularly near the beach region, kept us on our guard. Our route intercepted the Atlantic coast north of Myrtle Beach when we touched down at Sunset Beach just over the border. The area's activity ramped up even as our spent bodies clung to the only mode of transportation we'd need for the next month. Pacing oneself is an important principle, especially on a bicycle tour, one we had forgotten amid the excitement of new places with new faces.

A river in northeastern South Carolina

A long bridge connected the major portion of the community to the mainland. A narrow stretch of water and wetlands separated the two, where jet skiers were revving and reveling in their passionate pastime. The energy in the surroundings belied our fatigue. We enjoyed a satisfying entrée and a splendid view at a lunch spot overlooking the bridge. The timely meal would help curb our lethargy and boost us to an overnight stop in Shallotte.

The pace, though, was getting to us. Debbie's hands were going numb. After our honeymoon on wheels two summers prior, we both knew the feeling well. Hands aren't meant for the pressure of six or seven hours a day of constant leaning. We could muster only so many hand positions on our handlebars, and some positions could compromise control of the bicycle. Add in the tension of negotiating congested areas with sweaty palms, and our grips tended to tighten up. Hanging on too tightly was Debbie's dilemma. To be most effective in her cycling, she realized she needed to relax her hands.

The same can be true with life. When we hang on too tightly to possessions, people, or passions, pleasure can turn into pain, blessings to curses. Clinging to possessions can make us lose sight of the more important things in life, such as giving to others and cherishing our relationships. Smothering people can push them away, because they need the freedom to love us on their own terms. And being obsessive with what we truly enjoy can make the exciting become repetitive and boring. Even holding on too tightly to your occupation can prevent the growth and blessings that are waiting to unfold around the next bend in your career path.

What are you squeezing too tightly? Is it time to change things up? A few minor adjustments may relieve some of the pressure.

Maybe it's time to loosen your grip on some possessions. Have you ever considered blessing a child, sibling, niece, or nephew with a family treasure? You might find the joy of giving it away far surpasses the fatigue of clinging to it. Should you spend time with other people to give your closest acquaintances some space? You'll create enough stimulation to do everyone some good. And you may find the old relationships either improve or fade away as their season has long since come and gone. If you're tired of the same old routine, a new hobby is sure to add some spice to your life.

There's great value in letting go. When you do, you'll have room to accept the unexpected blessings that come your way.

. . . .

Do not lay up for yourselves treasures on earth, where moth and rust destroy and where thieves break in and steal; but lay up for yourselves treasures in heaven, where neither moth nor rust destroys and where thieves do not break in and steal.

MATTHEW 6:19-20

. . . .

Personal REFLECTION:

1. Do you own something that would mean more to someone else than it does to you? Why not give it away?

2. Is there something you can't let go of, and your grip is beginning to feel unhealthy? What steps can you take to release it? Who can show you how?

3. When you think about the most treasured relationship in your life, have you given that person the same freedom he or she has given you to realize all that God has in store? If not, what can you do to give that person some space?

LESSON 19

Restraints or Helpful Guidelines?

What may seem restrictive can actually protect
you from straying off course and keep you from harm.

BY TIM

O n day twenty-eight of the Mom-to-Mom Tour, we enjoyed a
long descent into Hunt Valley and lovely accommodations
in central Maryland, but the following morning we paid the
price. In the first several miles, we moved from a busy commuter road
outside of Baltimore to back roads with killer hills.

We continued into horse country, where we enjoyed a beautiful
respite from the climbing drudgery. Pastures as big and untamed as
open country meadows looked like golf fairways, with their lush, green,
manicured appearance. However, the encompassing wood-slatted fences,
often painted bright white to accentuate the scenery, suggested intruders
were more likely to step on horse droppings than golf balls. Those fences
were elegant in their simplicity and their surroundings. The picture-book
ambiance was quintessential Victorian.

Maryland forest

The inviting horse corrals were in stark contrast to the cold, padlock-clad, chain-link fences we had seen elsewhere. Those were designed to secure property and to restrain angry "muscle dogs" bred with aggression. Harsh, homegrown trainers had treated them with a steady dose of cruelty to heighten fear in passersby and would-be intruders, who would walk large arcs around the grounds of these menacing mutts. Snarling lips and grisly barks from lunging dogs will do that to you whether or not they are confined.

The wooden pasture fences reminded me of boundaries that God provides for our benefit. You've probably heard some of them: *Don't kill, don't steal, don't lie, don't have sex with anyone other than your spouse, don't cuss, etc.* Then there's the all-encompassing kind with a positive spin: *Do unto others as you would have them do unto you,* and *Love God with all you have within you.* Rather than restraining us, those "fences" offer freedom. They keep us from getting lost in uninhabitable terrain. They protect us so we can enjoy our surroundings, just as the shiny-coated horses with flowing manes could roam within their safe havens free from attack, with caretakers nearby to maintain their health and beauty.

The steel-caged fences we'd seen in days gone by resembled the entrapments people put themselves into when they listen to the voice of temptation. Those fences don't allow people to roam freely. Instead of respecting—and enjoying—the boundaries God lovingly offers them, guidelines to protect them and to help them grow, they become prisoners of their own bad choices.

We've heard about such entrapments firsthand with youth on TheHopeLine. Parents victimized by the sins of their parents cast their anger and hate onto their children, perpetuating a cycle of abuse that poisons families for generations. They remain chained to their destructive patterns through substance abuse or an insatiable lust that tragically knows no bounds. Neither parents nor children can break the curse, since they've not discovered the boundaries that offer freedom, or have been unwilling to roam within them. Youth caught in these cages may inflict self-harm—or worse—to escape. We also hear sad stories of the consequences of sex before marriage: unwanted pregnancies, confusion in the wake of "sex and run" episodes, and heart-wrenching emotional pain from breakups of relationships consummated too soon.

When we see the friendly confines that free as restraints to limit pleasure and self-fulfillment, prison walls close in on us from every side. Before realizing what has happened, we must struggle to break free. It's best not to wander in the first place, to avoid the difficult task of finding an escape after you've become shackled.

We left horse country and its inspirational promptings by midday with this important lesson: graze in pastures that bring life not death, and respect the boundaries God provides for your betterment. He provides them because He loves us and wants the best for us. He also knows we are prone to wander.

Before you choose where to graze, can you distinguish pasturelands with protective fences from those that bind you? It's not easy to pick the right boundaries when you don't know them, can't recall them, or have difficulty recognizing them. Understanding where you should and shouldn't roam is a process, because we're usually distracted with what we think are more important or more pleasurable matters. Yet realizing the importance of life-giving pastures and investing the time to discover them is a sign of true wisdom. You'll find ample guidance by reading the Bible and by listening to people who know what it says.

> **For this is the love of God, that we keep His commandments.**
> **And His commandments are not burdensome.**
>
> 1 JOHN 5:3

Personal REFLECTION:

1. How did you feel the last time you broke a rule designed to protect you?
2. When you think of boundaries, do you view them as restrictive or protective?
3. Consider talking to someone who you believe understands the Bible and ask him or her to show you some passages that describe some of God's protective boundaries.

LESSON 20

Moving Meditation

Immersing yourself in a peaceful setting will help you
get in touch with what really matters.

BY DEBBIE

Months before TheHopeLine Tour, I had started attending a
guided meditation group that met bi-weekly to allow partic-
ipants to unwind from the frenetic pace of life. This meditation group focused on connecting on a deeper level with the God of the
Bible rather than on any "inner self," as some groups teach. I had noticed
a considerable improvement in my serenity from some practical advice
shared by the group leader, Mary. Effective breathing is helpful in lowering
stress and anxiety. Mary taught me to breathe in for five seconds, hold it
for five seconds, and exhale for five seconds. It really does relax me. If I
repeat this exercise three to five times, I always feel calmer afterward. We
seldom pay attention to our breathing, but we wouldn't be here without it!

When bicycling, taking deep breaths increases my strength and
endurance. Climbing hills is much easier that way. Any form of physical

exertion requires deeper breathing so the blood can circulate more oxygen throughout the body.

On day nineteen of our tour, Tim and I engaged in a sort of moving meditation. As we pedaled rhythmically along Idaho's Lochsa River, we were mesmerized. The sound of the rushing river and the creeks that poured into it, the deep green conifers, and the clear blue sky were so relaxing that we fell into a meditative state. Despite the gradual incline for most of the day as we closed in on 5,235-foot Lolo Pass, the entrancing surroundings removed all distractions and allowed peace to flood our souls.

Lochsa River in Clearwater National Forest in Idaho

The beauty of our moving meditation was that it lasted all day long. Often, when we bicycle, we ride beside water, but never for an entire day. We stopped often enough to shoot over one hundred pictures and videos—and to indulge ourselves in the tranquility. We were alone yet together. Our stops were as calm as the setting. We were so connected with nature's voice and with one another that we remained silent to avoid disrupting the heavenly vibes. Being quiet never felt so good! We didn't even notice our sore rear ends, because we were so happy and relaxed, soaking in the scenery at every angle.

Our joy was heightened even more because we had journeyed there before. The prior evening, we had stayed at a small motel in Lowell, Idaho, with an adjoining restaurant where we had stopped for lunch on our first tour four years earlier. At this very site, Tim and I had conversed with a retired college professor about survival in the wild. Riding US Route 12 along the Lochsa River had been such a memorable part of that trip.

Revisiting the area brought those incredible memories back to life, with all of our senses activated as we rode. The sights, sounds, and scents drowned out the daily rigors of life on the road. The rushing water, the birds singing along the route, and the smell of sage and pine took our tour to a new level. Not to be outdone, the taste of ice-cold water and the touch of the warm sun on my skin added their own form of refreshment. On a tour filled with so many wonderful days, that day was among the best of TheHopeLine Tour. Following a few rough days of climbing and heat, we were grateful for distraction-free riding amid the cooler temperatures and the sensory overload.

Sometimes, we're brought to a place where we can ponder matters of the heart without everyday life getting in the way. We may intend to go there or we may stumble upon it, such as we did on that particular day. If you can seek out those places periodically, you'll have more opportunity to consider the things that matter most, such as faith, family, and friends. Some people may travel to a spot that has become special to them, where they can get away from life's distractions, think, and maybe even pray. Others connect with their thoughts and feelings when meeting with other like-minded people—for example, with a group of friends or at church. Still others are able to find solace in their home every morning when they enjoy a quiet time with God. And some people may come face-to-face with themselves when an unexpected setting or circumstance changes their focus. Regardless of their form, pursuing these opportunities for deeper engagement with life will deepen your commitment to the very objects of your meditation.

Come aside by yourselves to a deserted place and rest a while.

MARK 6:31A

Personal REFLECTION:

1. Do you periodically set aside a time and a place to consider the deeper things of life? If not, how might you find room for this in your life?

2. Ask someone you admire if he or she purposely sets aside a quiet time to consider God, family, or friends. How does that person make it happen?

3. Where is the best place, and when is the best time, for you to pursue peace?

LESSON 21

Balancing Act

Balance is essential to any successful pursuit.

BY TIM

Debbie and I had started our tour of the Atlantic coast aggressively despite the intense heat and humidity. What kind of weather would you expect for mid-July in Florida? And what were we thinking...or were we thinking? Our exuberance in unleashing our second long-distance tour—and in flat terrain with the potential for cycling many miles a day—had clouded good judgment and begun to wear us down physically. Our fifty-four-year-old bodies were not adapting well to the increased exertion and repetitive motion. I'd developed some nasty saddle sores.

We knew from experience that these early-tour injuries could pose problems and threaten the ride for weeks if not treated with respect. In our tour two years prior, the constant rubbing and chafing from long miles in the saddle had stricken both of us with wounds. Add in stickier air and steamier heat, and we had an even more hazardous formula for sores and tired muscles. We needed some time to recover. We also had other matters to address, including some editing on a writing project. Multitasking can be difficult when you're riding a bicycle.

Regardless, we cycled for our fifth straight day so we could rest on Sunday. That way, we could attend church without feeling like we were forfeiting cooler early-morning riding time. We'd try to maximize the mileage on Saturday with the upcoming rest day in clear view. With this backdrop, a glaring object lesson from nature drove home the need to slow down.

We crossed paths with two coastal birds, spotting them in front of a home to our right. We had arrived just in time for their matinee performance and decided to take in the show. They were walking in step at their own comfortable pace with no apparent reason to hurry. Watching them reminded us of our own togetherness and the marriage relationship, in which two individuals choose to walk through life together.

These herons sauntered together across two lawns. Then, they ventured ever so slowly into the roadway, seemingly without concern. They continued to amble along, which forced an oncoming motorist rounding the curve to slow down at the risk of an unsuspecting and less attentive motorist rear-ending him. Yet the carefree—and careless—birds continued their stroll across the road undeterred until they stepped into the obscurity of some brush. They weren't about to allow man-made mayhem to dictate their pace.

These birds had just walked out a profound truth. It's easy to allow the pace of life around you to fluster you and derail your activities, but it needn't. Slowing down, although challenging, is often necessary to walk with purpose.

We could relate to a harried pace. We'd been so excited to chew up the flat miles in Florida that we had forgotten to pace ourselves. We'd become ineffective and would have been unable to proceed unless we slowed down. As it turned out, we needed an extended break so my sore bum could heal.

Togetherness, at their own pace

We arrived at a motel on US Route 1 just north of Daytona Beach, at the end of a desolate, thirty-mile stretch. Within walking distance, we discovered a church with a ten o'clock Sunday morning service, a Dairy Queen, and several stores and restaurants. We'd arrived at an optimal rest stop where we crashed for a few days, caught up on other matters, and then continued on our way with rejuvenated vigor.

Balance is an important principle in life, just as it is in riding a bicycle. If you don't maintain balance at all times on a bicycle, you risk toppling over. It may be fun to ride on the edge, but you'll go down quickly and unexpectedly before you can avoid catastrophe. Once you've crashed, you're bound to incur some damage to yourself and maybe even to your bicycle. It may take quite some time to recover. And one of those times, you may do permanent damage.

When you lose your balance in life, you also risk damage and a protracted recovery time. It's much easier to cope with life if you stay in control and aim for a steady ride. For example, if you work too much, your productivity will decline. Your safety may be compromised, and you may receive less enjoyment from what you're doing. Reversing this trend may be difficult, because you or others might have become dependent upon the results of your labor. You'll pay too high a price when you ignore your family and friends. On other fronts, spending all of your time on meaningless tasks or simply living it up won't allow you the satisfaction and reward that accomplishments can bring to you and your loved ones.

We all have choices to make in how we manage our lives. Allowing your surroundings to determine your actions or the speed at which you execute them may ultimately slow your progress and reduce your effectiveness. Rather than succumbing to external pressures or simply using poor judgment, when you conduct your life judiciously and in accordance with the way you are wired—and in the best interests of you, your family, and others around you—then you can maximize your contributions to others and your own fulfillment.

When it seems as though life is about to steamroll you, perhaps it's time to unplug and regroup. We all operate on our own built-in clock. If you try to run according to someone else's, you may find yourself careening down a treacherous mountain pass with your front wheel about to come off. Slow down to maintain balance and complete the ride. You'll enjoy it much more that way, and you'll arrive soon enough.

The plans of the diligent lead surely to plenty, but those of everyone who is hasty, surely to poverty.

PROVERBS 21:5

Personal REFLECTION:

1. Are you managing your life, or is your life managing you?

2. Are you accomplishing many things with mediocrity or fewer things with excellence?

3. Have you ever been in a position where reckless behavior jeopardized other matters in your life? How did it make you feel? How might you manage your life differently so this doesn't happen again?

LESSON 22

Another Form of Compassion

Recognizing our limitations and focusing our attention
in those areas where we can really make a difference
will help us progress on the road ahead.

BY TIM

Debbie and I had the services of TheHopeLine forefront in our minds as we embarked on the tour that bore its name. That tour would be more than just an adventure or a pleasure ride. We were committed to making a difference for the organization and the young people it serves. So, when we rolled into town on the third day in search of the local Super 8 motel and passed the Eugene Christian Fellowship in Springfield, Oregon, we suspected it might be more than a coincidence. Springfield would provide plenty of services while we took a break from cycling. And a church within walking distance fit well for the Sunday morning to follow.

Nearly two miles down the road, we arrived within spitting distance of our destination for the evening. A walk across the street would bring us to the front door.

Then, as we prepared to cross the busy intersection, there he was: a young man, seemingly under the influence, with a bag of belongings and a cardboard sign upon which he'd scrawled his hard-luck story. The details weren't needed to understand that not all was well.

He was collecting funds in a small container from any willing donors who passed by. He seemed too young for that trip. An older man alongside him appeared to have walked the same path, which made it awkward to engage the younger man one on one.

As Debbie and I awaited the tick-tock of the walk signal, I rummaged through my handlebar bag in search of a card that would connect him to TheHopeLine. In some respects, opening the handlebar bag seemed counterintuitive, since it also contained valuables. Thoughts went through my head about the vulnerability Debbie and I shared as bicycle tourists. Yet our lot was much different from his. We had everything we needed, including our next meal, contentment, one another, and peace with God. He was obviously down and out, angry, and appeared to be panhandling, but who was I to judge?

Regardless, when the pedestrian walk signal appeared, Debbie moved toward more comfortable surroundings on the other side of the street, while I lingered to share the card with the young man and to instruct or encourage him, should the opportunity arise.

"Here," I said, as I handed him the card. "They'll help you. Just give them a call."

I knew he could afford a toll-free call at a payphone. Just a few seconds earlier, another compassionate soul had shared some of her bounty with him from the three-inch crack in her car window; he'd run to her offering and gobbled it up like an undernourished pet whose owner had just returned home to feed it. Mine was another form of compassion. TheHopeLine approach is often one of tough love. If you have the compulsion to get better or you can't find your way and just need a nudge in the right direction, then TheHopeLine can help you— and its coaches want to do just that.

As I turned to make my way across the busy street, I encouraged him again: "Give them a call. They'll help you."

"I don't want to hear nothing about Jesus. I've had it with that," was his venomous reply. He was obviously angry and would need some help to unravel that when he was ready. I wasn't sure how he connected TheHopeLine with God, but he did.

"Just tell them that when you call," I said. "They'll still help you."

Seconds later, I had crossed the street. I began to wonder if Debbie or I would talk or chat with him online soon—or whether his anger would prevent him from reaching out for help that could truly change his situation.

Should I have done more? The thought nagged me afterward.

We can't be all things to all people. Sometimes, we have an opportunity to intervene in someone's life and make a real difference. Other times, we are ill-equipped, or the person in need of help is not ready to accept it. We may become the undeserving recipient of some misdirected wrath while bringing that person no closer to a solution—and maybe even further away from it. At still other times, it's difficult to know whether or not we can help.

Thankfully, we're responsible to God alone and not for those on the other end of our random encounters. If we can develop the ability to see with His eyes and hear with His ears, we'll be better able to discern whether or not the time is right to offer help. Simply communicating that you care may be all the help you can offer—and exactly what the individual needs. Regardless, rest assured that when you walk away, you'll have another chance with someone else just down the road when it's clear the time is right. When in doubt, save yourself for that next encounter. Otherwise, you may risk doing more harm than good. God has someone else lined up to help the person in need at the appointed time. Meanwhile, pray that the person will be ready to accept the help he or she so desperately needs.

> Do not give what is holy to the dogs; nor cast your
> pearls before swine, lest they trample them under their feet,
> and turn and tear you in pieces.
>
> MATTHEW 7:6

Personal REFLECTION:

1. What strengths do you have to offer to the world around you?

2. Think about the desire you have to help others. Now consider the need that exists as compared with your ability to meet that need. How might you apply your strengths to meeting some of those needs?

3. When was the last time you had an opportunity to intervene in someone else's life? Did you help that person out of your gifting, or did you get in over your head? If the latter, what can you do differently the next time?

LESSON 23

One Lost Puppy

Even though you can't solve the world's problems all by
yourself, seizing an opportunity to help someone in need
enhances your own journey.

BY TIM

I'll never forget a mystery dog that found us along the roadside
in Kentucky. During a rest break, Debbie and I had wheeled our
bicycles off the road onto a steep and narrow side road, one we
knew would see little to no traffic. We were eating a snack when, all of
a sudden, we heard some noise in the thick woods nearby. Moments
later, out came a puppy, as if he had just squeezed out of his mother's
womb! He was so excited to see us that he tinkled uncontrollably on the
road as he wiggled his body around and yelped. Obviously, his "barker"
was not yet fully developed.

The dog might have been pit bull or a close relative. His sudden
appearance was unusual, because homes were nowhere in sight.
Furthermore, he had worked his way through a wire fence to see us.
We'd heard of wild dogs in Kentucky, but this puppy was as far away

from our perception of a wild dog as could be. This dog was lovable and without an ounce of aggression. He was clearly a lost puppy, one who looked hungry and in need of love, if not downright pathetic.

One lost puppy

We've come to appreciate that you don't want to befriend dogs you meet while bicycling. They will follow you and endanger you or themselves in the process. So, we chose not to feed or pet the dog, even though he was tugging at our heartstrings with his oh so puppy-dog eyes, his yips, and his obvious gestures for a portion of our snacks. Even so, when we started down the road, he chased Debbie for a half mile while two cars negotiated around the two of them. Finally, he realized we weren't adopting him, so he gave up.

Later, I found myself comparing that dog to many of the youth who reach out to TheHopeLine. Both have no one else to turn to, and they are in dire need of help. Sure, many of these youth belong to families, but they may be as neglected as those without parents. While most parents love their children and do the best they can to improve their lives, some parents have lost their way, and their kids pay the price. Those parents may be in the other room on the computer looking at porn, chatting on the phone with a romantic interest for hours on end, or under the influence of drugs or alcohol, ready to lash out when their child competes for their attention. Debbie and I hear some sad stories on TheHopeLine.

I've thought about how we treated our little lost puppy. We couldn't very well have stuffed him in a pannier and carted him around with us. Yet we prolonged his misery, because we didn't help him.

When someone reaches out to TheHopeLine, he or she won't be ignored if someone is there to pick up the phone or respond to the chat. However, if no one is available to answer the cry for help, someone who reaches out will receive the same treatment as our little lost puppy received from us. They'll go looking for help elsewhere. Maybe they'll get some, or maybe they will become embittered and repeat the sins of their angry or depressed parents. Our surprise visitor would develop a much different disposition if someone who chose to abuse him and make him angry, rather than love him, took him in. Then, he'd be the type of wild dog we had imagined before entering Kentucky.

Just as the little lost puppy needed help, so do thousands of people in our world who have nowhere else to turn. And because they're people, the call to help them comes with higher stakes. Just as Debbie and I were limited in what assistance we could provide the stray puppy, so too are most of us limited in meeting the overwhelming needs among our fellow man. Regardless, we can still make a difference. Everyone has some measure of the three Ts: time, talent, and treasure. As opportunities present themselves, you'll know from which you should give.

Although the aggregate suffering of our fellow man exceeds what each one of us alone can fix, much less comprehend, each of us can help reduce the anguish. The next time you encounter someone in need, resolve to do what you sense God is asking of you. You can help by donating money to worthy organizations or you can give your time by volunteering at a local shelter, church, or mission. You can also love and assist people who are already in your life, such as family, neighbors, and friends. Lives are hanging in the balance. Are you going to turn away, or will you join the many others who have already decided to help?

Learn to do good; seek justice, rebuke the oppressor; defend the fatherless, plead for the widow.

ISAIAH 1:17

Personal REFLECTION:

1. When you see someone in need, does it make you feel angry, sad, or compassionate?

2. Think of someone you know who is struggling. Regardless of what brought that person to his or her present state, imagine how difficult it must be for that person to cope with the circumstances.

3. What is one practical way you can help this person without demeaning or judging him or her?

SECTION

IV

Finding Motivation

After you've prepared adequately, made the necessary adjustments, and taken wise precautions, you may still find it difficult to make progress. Unexpected developments can lead to discouragement. You might have become stuck, or you may be struggling between the forces of fear and faith.

The stories in this section will demonstrate you're not alone in your struggles. Rather than losing hope, be encouraged. You can get moving at a healthy pace once again.

SECTION IV TAKEAWAYS
Things to Encourage and Motivate Me

1.

2.

3.

4.

5.

LESSON 24

Facing Fear

Fear of the unknown can cripple your efforts to make
progress. It's important to remember these two words
found throughout the Holy Bible: "Fear not!"

BY TIM

When we awoke one morning at Gateway Wilderness
Campground in Idaho, the mysteries of the dark and those
of the deep woods of the Clearwater National Forest, along
with our fears of the creatures of the night, had vanished. We found
ourselves intact, just as we'd been the day before. Gingerly, we crawled
out of our overnight cocoon. Rather than a wet washcloth to awaken us,
the heavy condensation on our tent covering slapped us in the face. The
next challenge, with its associated mysteries of the unknown, was about
to do the same. Neither of us, it seemed, was in a hurry to move on.

Lolo Pass lay ahead. A fellow camper had told us about it. Speaking
with someone who had been through the pass before and had chosen
to ride through it again was comforting, despite the fact he was thirty
years younger than us. However, we could take no other comfort from

our conversation. His references to more of the logging trucks we had seen the day before didn't help matters. Neither did his comments about a narrow road with plenty of switchbacks. Pedaling up a mountain pass with a fully loaded touring bicycle was a new experience for us. We had no idea what to expect.

Fueled by his scant description, my doubts and anxiety morphed into outright fear. Thoughts ran amuck in my head: *How narrow is the road? How much traffic will crowd us to the edge and present us with a balancing nightmare atop bulky bicycles? Will the wind at higher altitude buffet our loads? Just how steep will portions of this be? Will we be able to handle this climb? Assuming we make it all the way to the top, how hair-raising is the descent down the other side?*

We took four hours to leave the campsite. Normally, Debbie couldn't wait to get going in the morning. Clearly, she was stalling. I wasn't prepared to confront the next leg of our journey either. As with all endeavors, though, embarking on them tends to reduce the anxiety as specific tasks begin to occupy your mind. Such was the case for us when we finally left.

After forty miles of relatively easy climbing alongside the peaceful and picturesque Lochsa River, we arrived at Lochsa Lodge in Powell for lunch. We gathered ourselves and replenished food and fluids for the stiffer climb ahead. The beautiful accommodations provided a welcome escape from the wilderness outside, suggesting the backcountry would not continue indefinitely.

We departed with renewed vigor and began to work our way up the mountain pass. The road narrowed and began to curl around the mountain, just as last night's neighbor had described. Trucks and motor-cycles sped around the curves like nobody's business, like they belonged there and we didn't. We protected our own narrow space near the ever-diminishing shoulder as the ascent steepened. There was no turning back or stopping now. We would never be able to start from a dead stop on this incline. Sightseeing was also a bad idea. Although inviting vistas beckoned, we needed to concentrate on steadying our loads on this treacherous roadway. We were one rubberneck away from an accident we couldn't afford in this remote setting.

As we crawled up the road, we met curve after curve and dispatched each one with the slow persistence of cyclists who knew no other way. The curves and the road were challenging, given the traffic, but the grade was not. Furthermore, the steep, adjacent drop-offs I had imagined did not exist. That was just as well, because we had plenty of other things to deal with. Soon, however, a road sign signaled our near arrival at the top. We were about to slay this dragon, just as we had the mysteries of the dark the night before.

Somehow, our arrival at the summit was anticlimactic. The Lolo Pass Visitor Center was closed. No one was around. The long shadows and the unmistakable chill of dusk meant the sun would be setting soon. We had tarried too long at our morning campsite, and now we were paying the price.

Fear of the unknown often surpasses the reality of what we will encounter. Our mind plays tricks on us, creating what seem like insurmountable barriers between us and our destination. Until we decide to move forward, fear cannot be unmasked. Rather, it grows into an even larger specter, threatening to clamp us in place.

Our ride up Lolo Pass had exposed fear as a fraud. Once again, the shadow of fear had been far more intimidating than the experience itself. The physical challenge was the least of our struggle. We needed that lesson, because we needed the emerging confidence for the three thousand miles still ahead on our honeymoon tour.

The battle with fear, however, never ends. It lurks with the unknowns that lie ahead. No sooner had we rendered another anxiety powerless than others equally adept at freezing us in place fell like the cool of the evening. At least now we could recognize them for what they were before they took control.

Fear and its constant companion, anxiety, are insidious foes battling for supremacy in our mind, aiming to block progress to parts unknown, to prevent wondrous adventures ahead, and to stunt the personal growth that will turn us into the people God intends. The encounter will come with a struggle, but it can also come with a deep sense of fulfillment and satisfaction.

There's a place in your mind for fear, but it doesn't belong between you and your goals and dreams. Rather, it should occupy a room in the recesses of your mind and be allowed to come out periodically to provide relevant cautions. Allow it to prompt you to make adjustments on your journey, but don't allow it to send you home with your tail between your legs. Check the reading on your "fear-o-meter" from time to time. If it is rising above the boiling point, it's time for another adventure, with your Pilot by your side, to put fear back in its rightful place.

Fear not, for I am with you; be not dismayed, for I am your God. I will strengthen you, yes, I will help you, I will uphold you with My righteous right hand.

ISAIAH 41:10

Personal REFLECTION:

1. In what area of your life does fear tend to grip you?

2. Why do you think that fear arises?

3. How can you continue to move ahead and work through your fear rather than allowing it to control you?

LESSON 25

Worrying

When we dwell on problems rather than seek encouragement and solutions, it's hard to move forward. Negative
thinking will kill our efforts every time.

BY TIM

It was hard to believe what had happened in such a short time as we began our first tour. Debbie and I had married two weeks earlier. We'd spent a few days on the Maine coast and then moved my belongings out of my apartment of twenty-five years. That was back in New England. On the fourth day of our grand escape in the Pacific Northwest, we were trying our hand at bicycle touring. I'd been stuck behind a desk for thirty years, so the radical change came as welcome relief, especially with Debbie by my side after so many years of waiting for female companionship.

Something happened out on I-84 on that day that I will never forget, much as I might like to. Cycling on the interstate may seem like an unusual place to choose to spend your honeymoon, but it was a necessary cost to move us through the beautiful Columbia River Gorge.

An incident that occurred there shook us to the core. I was sitting in the front row at that horror flick. And it served as a warning of just how high the cost of riding on the interstate—or any mistake on our journey—could be.

Trouble around the bend on I-84 in Oregon

As a tractor-trailer sped by, Debbie hit a rumble strip and lost her grip on the handlebars. Her front wheel began to swivel, which almost certainly should have caused her—or anyone else—to fall or swerve into the path of the dangerous traffic and…well…not to mince words, be run over and die an untimely death.

A seventeen-day marriage was not what I'd had in mind when I said, "I do" after fifty-two years as a single, but all I could do was watch helplessly as the monstrous eighteen-wheeler roared next to us and Debbie fought for control of the bicycle. At the last second, somehow, she clutched the handlebars and righted the heavy bike, even though both tires had fallen into deep ruts in the rumble strip. Miraculously, she pedaled straight out of the strip. I still don't know how she did it. She only weighs 120 pounds, and her loaded bicycle weighed about eighty.

That one event early in our tour had christened us. We had learned one of the severe risks of bicycle touring up close and personal. It took some time for me to shake the anxiety, to slow my heart rate to normal, and to swallow that persistent lump in my throat. No one can go through a near-miss experience like that without thinking about the potential consequences of bicycling on highways. Near misses will also test your resolve to continue and maybe even modify your approach.

Debbie and I were both determined to move on, wiser and better prepared. We wouldn't allow that test to stop our journey. We also didn't want to dwell on the potential hazards and allow trauma to rob us of the joy of our tour. There was too much of life to explore, and we'd waited far too long to discover it.

If you think too much about what might go wrong, you'll never get anywhere. When you dwell on problems, you are worrying. And worry can steal your joy. Worry points to an imbalance between fear and faith. It's like paying interest on a debt you don't owe, and it's a costly investment in something that may never happen. Keeping your concerns in proper perspective will prevent them from ruling your mental and emotional well-being—and your life. There's Someone who would like to ease your burden. He never meant for you to carry it alone.

For Debbie and me, tiptoeing through life, constantly scanning from side to side and looking behind, will not move us as swiftly or deftly to our destination. It will only compromise our journey. Instead, we'll try to make prudent decisions to equip and protect ourselves as best we know how. Then, we'll move forward with confidence, because we have a Guide with us, a Higher Power who "has our back." He straightens out our handlebars and powers our bicycles out of harm's way when we're not quite able to on our own. That unforgettable episode on I-84 was living proof.

Which of you by worrying can add one cubit to his stature?
MATTHEW 6:27

Personal REFLECTION:

1. When you think about what worries you most, how many of the scenarios you imagine have ever come true?

2. What is the most significant thing you worry about? As you consider it, imagine three possible positive outcomes. If you thought of them in less than thirty seconds, think of three more.

3. To whom can you talk confidentially about your worries?

LESSON 26

The Deception of Responsibility

When responsibilities that seem noble trump a higher
calling, you've been deceived into taking a wrong turn
in your journey.

BY TIM

Responsibility. It's a relative term. We all have our own definition of it, and our definition changes as we change. We can
shirk responsibility, bite off more than our fair share, or allow
it to consume us. I'd had such a strong sense of responsibility for the
several years that preceded our marriage that I knew of little else. So,
with plenty to go around, I offloaded some of it. After all, you can't
unload all of it and hope to achieve your calling…or keep satisfactory
relations with any of the people in your life.

Walla Walla, Washington, seemed like a friendly town of reasonable
size and an ideal place to catch up on some unfinished business. We
had put these responsibilities off long enough. We'd left the Columbia
River Gorge and the state of Oregon for good after six days of breaking
away from the old life. However, even a carefree honeymoon has its
everyday moments.

The time had arrived to fess up to our responsibilities. I placed a call to a board member of the company where I had worked for twenty-six years while Debbie called her sister to check up on family. My call was an obligatory formality, an exit interview to help those left behind. Debbie's, however, would be the weightier call. She discovered that her father had fallen and hit his head when returning home from our wedding. His fall had triggered some mini-strokes. When he picked up the phone, Debbie was not prepared for what she was about to hear.

As I was answering business questions on my call, I saw Debbie's face crumble at the sound of her father's slurred speech. She tried to hold things together for her father's ears, but she couldn't hold back the sniffles—or the anguished look on her face. Her reaction caused me concern. I wondered what type of news I would hear when we both ended our calls. I also wondered if we'd be making another call—to check airfares to Denver, where her father lived.

After we wrapped up our calls, we went into the convenience store to buy lunch and then sat outside to talk. In anticipation of the worst, Debbie had already queried her sister about her father's condition and had done the analysis. As much as she could draw a conclusion like this for an octogenarian with failing health, she had determined her father's condition was not imminently life-threatening. There was no compelling reason for our adventure to end prematurely. Besides, prayer knows no boundaries. We could bring our concerns to the One who knows us better than we know ourselves. His yoke is easy, and His burden is light.

We both had elderly parents who lived many miles away from us. It was simply a part of being fifty-something those days. The next time the phone rang, we might have heard troubling news. However, we wouldn't expect to hear the worst when we picked it up, and we weren't about to sit idly by the phone to wait for that inevitable call. If you live life on deathwatch for aging parents, then you may mourn your own death along with theirs. You risk translating concern into worry, and losing much joy in your own life in the process. Parents who truly love you don't want that for you.

Balancing act in Walla Walla, Washington

Life throws many concerns and responsibilities our way. We all have them. If you think you have it worse than others do, maybe you're overemphasizing the negative. Sometimes, what seems like the high road of responsibility is bent on throwing you off course. Responsibility may simply be an excuse to keep you mired in a comfortable setting, feeling secure with people and duties you know well. Yet binding yourself to responsibilities that have other caretakers waiting in the wings may be keeping you from a higher calling. Your higher calling may entail a higher degree of responsibility and instill fear, such as caring for a terminally ill parent, but a difficult calling will not feel burdensome to the called.

If God has placed a desire deep within you, do you think He wants you derailed with other "responsibilities"? Granted, you may need to take side trips and respites from your journey to address other duties from time to time, but He'll always make provision for you to pursue a higher calling. How many fruitful, rewarding, and uplifting activities do you miss because you are tending to things that don't really require your attention and leave you no closer to your destination than when you first considered pursuing it? If the truth be told, those responsibilities don't need you; you just can't let them go.

Then another of His disciples said to Him, "Lord, let me first go and bury my father." But Jesus said to him, "Follow Me, and let the dead bury their own dead."

MATTHEW 8:21-22

Personal REFLECTION:

1. How are certain responsibilities in your life preventing you from pursuing a more worthy calling?

2. What responsibilities do you own more than you should? What would happen if you backed away from them?

3. Whom can you ask to share or assume some of your responsibilities?

LESSON 27

Good Samaritans

Sometimes, God sends us help when we're having
trouble helping ourselves.

BY DEBBIE

The ride through upstate New York on our honeymoon tour was wonderful. We capped it off on the fifty-seventh day with eighty-odd miles through some beautiful but desolate stretches. We were in the midst of the Adirondacks, with plenty of forested hills and bodies of water. However, the final few miles on that day made the biggest impression of all.

After departing the village of North Hudson, we traveled many miles into early evening in anticipation of reaching Ticonderoga, where we believed we'd find a motel for the night. We knew we were headed in the right direction when we finally hit Route 74 and headed east. We figured we'd be in town before long. With the sun setting, we were pushing hard to reach services before nightfall. However, the longer we rode, the more we understood that we'd be cycling in the dark. Each turn in the road suggested the end might be near, but only more trees appeared, with an occasional roadside pond to break up the monotony.

I don't like riding after dark. It's scary enough in broad daylight to ride a road like that without any shoulders on it. Traffic was sparse, but most of the cars that came along were speeding. With a curvy road surrounded by trees at dusk, I wondered how much more difficult it would be for drivers to see us.

We cycled until the sun left us from behind. Then, with no town in sight, we pulled into a roadside turnoff to find our lights. It was so dark that we needed them to see where we were going, let alone to alert motorists we were on the roadway.

We hadn't used the lights much on that trip. We'd had many twilight rides, but nothing like the one we were on. I'd given Tim the lights after the last time we used them, but he didn't know where he'd put them. In fact, he thought I had them. As we continued to look for them, a middle-aged couple in an SUV pulled off the road and joined us at our rest stop.

"It's all downhill from here!" the man exclaimed. "You're a few miles from town, but you can coast from here. If you'd like, we'll follow you and shine our lights for you so you can see."

That man had just spoken the magic words. We accepted his offer instantly and closed up our panniers. There was no sense wasting any more time looking for lights in the dark. Those kind strangers knew more about the road ahead than we did. And they were offering to protect us along the way. That's all we needed to know.

Soon, we were off. We could feel the effects of the hill immediately. The grade was so steep that I had difficulty slowing my bicycle. My hands were weary, so I decided to simply enjoy the ride—and it was a thrill. Before long, we saw lights from the town, just as our Good Samaritans had promised.

Once at the bottom of the hill, we spotted a motel and pedaled toward it. Our guardian angels pulled up beside us. No sooner had we thanked them than they were gone. We didn't even get their names, but we'll never forget them.

I wonder what caused our Good Samaritans to pass our way precisely when we needed them most. Did they leave camp late? Had they just filled the car with gas down the road? Or were they hurrying home to watch a favorite show on television? What caused them to stop? And why did they decide to help us down the road, knowing we would slow them down and make them a potential obstacle for faster vehicles?

What we had just experienced defied explanation. We had received exactly what we needed right when we needed it. And we didn't even have to ask. When we were atop the hill preparing for a ride into town with headlamps, we had no idea what was ahead of us, nor could we see it. With such a steep hill and such a dark sky, we were in trouble without their help.

I've replayed that scene over and over since it occurred and considered what could have happened. What if a deer had darted out in front of me? What if I'd hit a nasty pothole and gone flying? What if I'd blown out a tire? At the time, I wasn't concerned, because our helpers made me feel safe—and the free fall was exhilarating!

It's comforting to know God sends the perfect helpers at just the right time. You needn't be afraid or worry when you trust in Him. Simply enjoy the ride!

But a certain Samaritan, as he journeyed, came where he was. And when he saw him, he had compassion.

LUKE 10:33

Personal REFLECTION:

1. Can you think of a time when a stranger came to your aid?

2. How did it make you feel?

3. How did you describe it at the time: as a chance encounter or a divine appointment? How about now?

LESSON 28

Passing a Test

A test run will often boost confidence, reduce fear's
grip, and unleash the capacity for greater gains.

BY TIM

After two consecutive rest days in Medina, Ohio, on
TheHopeLine Tour, the weather had turned cold. It felt like
we had skipped fall, with morning temperatures in the low
40s and "feels-like" readings in the 30s. We were in for a real test. We
knew we could handle heat, but what about riding in cold weather?
Frankly, the prospect itself was chilling, so this test was pivotal. With
cooler weather ahead as we marched deeper into fall, could we handle
riding in the cold temperatures?

I remember playing basketball outdoors in subzero weather as a
kid—and without mittens or gloves. Many days, I walked a mile to and
from school in subzero weather or blizzards. Being outside in crisp winter
weather was simply part of life in Houlton, Maine. I didn't mind it a bit.

Decades later, however, I didn't tolerate the cold as well. Losing some
body weight on that bicycle trip had made me even more susceptible to

cold temperatures. Even my hot-blooded wife was a bit concerned about how we would adapt to the cooler temperatures. When you bicycle, you create wind on your exposed skin. That airflow translates to wind chill. If you're cycling into a headwind, the effective wind speed increases, along with its chilling effect.

We didn't sleep well the prior night. We'd been glued to the weather forecasts and were dreading the biting cold predicted for our early-morning ride to church and the afternoon ride in well-below seasonal temperatures.

Prepping for the cold

I was as determined not to get cold as I was to finish that bicycle tour. I packed on six layers of clothing up top and four down below. With Debbie's naturally warm tendencies, she managed with less, although an impromptu visit to a bicycle shop in Peninsula and a strategic purchase of a pair of shoe coverings from the bargain bin helped rescue her cold toes.

Dressing warmly worked remarkably well. I even felt overheated at times as we passed through Cuyahoga Valley National Park. We felt liberated and justified to cycle to our hearts' content even while the mercury struggled to touch 50 degrees in the "heat" of the afternoon.

That day's ride was a confidence booster. Passing a test always feels good. We wouldn't be intimidated by cold-weather riding any longer.

Our arrival at First Baptist Church in Medina also encouraged us. Unlike the temperature outside, the people were warm and engaging. In fact, it felt like they'd been waiting for us. While we had focused on how we might fare bicycling in colder weather, little did we know we were in for another type of test.

After explaining our mission at the front door, the greeter escorted us to the youth pastor, who invited us to share a brief plug for TheHopeLine to his senior high group later in the morning. In the meantime, we attended a small group Bible study, where the facilitator invited us to share our mission with that class.

Our visit to the youth group exposed us to a guest speaker's presentation about missions work in Pakistan. After his talk, the group heard our two-minute spiel. My pitch was indeed a test. The group was much larger than others we had shared with farther west. Furthermore, this group consisted entirely of youth, to whom the TheHopeLine targets its services.

My explanation of TheHopeLine went smoothly until I was about to recite its phone number. Suddenly, I blanked out! I couldn't think of the number.

Thankfully, my clever wife added an important visual to the presentation, right on cue. Debbie turned around to show the entire group—and me—TheHopeLine's phone number on the back of her T-shirt: 1-800-394-4673. I'd recited that number from memory many times—although never in front of a hundred youth. I love our T-shirts—and my wife!

The next presentation to a large youth group would be easier. Learning by doing is the best confidence builder. Some call it "baptism by fire." All I knew was that we could do it.

Given the hubbub on that day, we didn't realize we were about to eclipse a mileage milestone, even though we'd bicycled only thirty-four miles. When I recorded the mileage at the end of the day, we learned we'd cycled over four thousand miles on TheHopeLine Tour. That milestone felt like a special reward for passing the tests of that ninety-fifth day of the tour. We'd achieved a mileage goal set at the start of our trip, which was satisfying. If we could cycle eight hundred more miles home, we'd really be celebrating. We could do it!

His lord said to him, "Well done, good and faithful servant; you have been faithful over a few things, I will make you ruler over many things. Enter into the joy of your lord."

MATTHEW 25:23

Personal REFLECTION:

1. First-time experiences can be challenging. When was the last time you started a new endeavor? Was it easier when you did it the second time?

2. Schedule a time this week to practice a skill you need to improve.

3. If you are experiencing some anxiety and fear about an upcoming challenge, what kind of test run can you orchestrate to build your confidence?

LESSON 29

Don't Stop Now

The best way to deal with being stuck is to avoid it in the
first place, even when the going gets tough.

BY TIM

Route 185 from Sullivan to Potosi, Missouri, on the edge of
the Ozark region, lived up to its billing during TheHopeLine
Tour. It was the toughest road we'd faced for weeks. After
thirty-five miles, we were happy to say we'd made it through
unscathed. Not only did the road lack shoulders, it also had stretches
where we couldn't leave it without crashing into a gully or the woods.

Motorists were thoughtful and cautious when they spotted our
wide loads ambling up the steep hills. Most were gracious, giving us
plenty of space and time to ascend. Once atop the hill, they could
see oncoming traffic and swerve into the other lane to pass us when
the coast was clear.

We climbed almost four thousand feet of elevation that day. I
must admit, though, we rather enjoyed some of the descents. That

stretch had some rollers that we climbed with little effort due to the pitch of the preceding hill's descent. Among the modest rolling hills, however, were more challenging grades. Although we had to exercise caution due to the narrow road, we had fun. Once we left the forest, beautiful views of the neighboring countryside glistened and danced atop the panoramic hills.

Cyclists beware!

One killer hill was so steep that I wondered whether I would need to dismount the bike and walk it. I was determined to make it to the crest, though, because I knew from experience that cycling is faster than walking, even when you're crawling up a steep grade at only three miles per hour. That particular hill was deceptive, because a curve in the road disguised the magnitude of the climb ahead. We had just plummeted down a steep grade and crossed a river. As we rounded the curve and began to climb out of the gulley, we noticed that the road went up, up, up! Our leg muscles began to burn due to the incline.

If you're unable to anticipate hills like that soon enough, your bicycle will be in too high a gear for you to pedal. By the time you shift into a lower gear, you'll have lost any of the momentum you were carrying from the slope you just went down. If you don't stop or fall over, you'll have to generate all of the power needed to stay upright from a near standstill. That's not easy with a heavy load on a steep grade. Sometimes, it doesn't matter if you can see the length and pitch of a hill. An extreme incline tests even the strongest of cyclists.

Fortunately, I was able to shift gears in time to keep moving. With a great deal of exertion, I propelled the bicycle all the way to the top of the hill, pedal stroke by long, slow pedal stroke. The hill had perhaps the steepest grade we'd encountered on the entire tour.

My sweet wife, however, was not as fortunate. Sometimes, Debbie would cycle from side to side on roads with severe pitch and use more of the pavement to climb the hill. In essence, she would allow her stamina and her strong heart to come to the aid of her stressed leg muscles. On that day, however, that plan backfired.

A car met us on the hill at precisely the wrong time. Debbie was on the left side of the road and had to pull off the road and stop to avoid getting run over. Once she had stopped, she couldn't remount the bicycle and resume pedaling on the steep grade, so she had to walk her bicycle. Even with her entire body on the job, she had trouble pushing the weight uphill, and the process took much longer than pedaling.

When you're in the midst of a trying task, it demands as much concentration and determination as it does ability. Stopping in the middle of it will often make it more difficult to accomplish, let alone resume. You've interrupted a concerted effort, and it's hard to bring the necessary forces back in unison. You may need to resort to less efficient and more costly means. Whenever possible, muster all of the strength and courage you can to complete the challenge. Even if you have to change tactics, as Debbie did, press on toward the goal. Although it may stretch your limits, you'll be better for it once you reach the top of that hill. You'll have a fresh perspective from there, and you'll be able to proceed on your journey with renewed confidence.

- -

Let us run with endurance the race that is set before us.

HEBREWS 12:1B

- -

Personal REFLECTION:

1. Think of a time when you gave up on a difficult task. Were you able to accomplish it eventually? If so, do you think it required more effort than if you had persevered in the first place?

2. Think of a time when a task became more difficult but you stuck with it. Describe the sense of accomplishment you felt when you finished it.

3. What can you do today to remind yourself not to give up the next time the going gets tough? As part of this exercise, consider setting goals and measuring yourself against them.

LESSON 30

Stuck Fast

Sometimes, complications stymie efforts to make progress. If you're stuck, consider asking someone for help. That person may see something you don't and have you on your way quicker than you can imagine.

BY TIM

Gillette, Wyoming, was the site of one of the more bizarre bicycle repair problems I have ever seen. We had just finished cleaning our chains in the motel parking lot after checking out when two fourth-graders on bicycles came over to ask us for help. One of them had gotten himself into a pickle. He was carrying a cloth shopping bag with a bottle of water in it. The bag and bottle were caught in the front brake assembly on his bicycle. The boys asked us to rescue them, because they didn't know what to do.

I had never seen anything quite like that before. The water bottle was stuck fast between the rim and the brake pad. I thought the best remedy might be to release some of the water from the bottle to relieve the pressure against the rim. I reached into the bag, unscrewed the cap, and let some water out. Almost immediately, the bottle came free, and the bag came with it. What remained was to deal with the consequences of the mishap. The brake had become misaligned, and one of its pads was rubbing against the rim. We delegated that issue to a neighbor, who no doubt knew more about how to fix it than we did.

The boys were grateful. We handed them a business card and invited them to follow our trip across country online. They were excited, and it made our day.

I thought about that incident as Debbie and I headed down I-90. It reminded me of interactions we'd had with youth on TheHopeLine.

Like the two boys, youth come to TheHopeLine because they're stuck, and they don't know what to do about it. They're in over their heads. When people find themselves in that position, they're usually ready to ask for help—and to accept it.

Oftentimes, the client needs to release emotion, frustration, and anxiety before addressing collateral issues. Once the pressure eases, the solution to the primary problem ignites, and we can assign the cleanup to someone with the right skills.

Meanwhile, a squishy feeling in my back tire—and the accompanying sick feeling in my stomach—rudely interrupted my train of thought about the youngsters we had helped. Seven miles down the interstate, I had sustained my second flat tire of the trip. It was the rear tire, so fixing the flat would be more involved. The repair job cost us an hour, which would have consequences later in the day.

After lunch in Moorcroft, the forecasted storms reared their ugly thunderheads from the southwest. Lightning danced on the horizon as motorcyclists on standby joined us in contemplating next steps. Debbie and I were to head southeast, and the sky in that direction looked good. We decided to go for it.

Three miles down the road, darkness closed in from the southwest. The wind was blowing toward the northeast, with the storm threatening to intercept us. If we cycled fast enough toward the brighter southeastern sky, we might avoid the storm.

Debbie and I put in perhaps our fastest twenty miles yet. However, we were losing the battle. At one juncture, lightning struck the ground a few hundred yards to our left. Its deafening clap of thunder called us to attention, and we realized we had gotten ourselves into a pickle, just like the boys we'd met at the start of our day. Soon, we felt large drops of water smack us from the west. As we sped toward cover in Upton, a frenzied pronghorn joined us from just off the shoulder as if racing us. In its confusion, it suddenly reversed course. Even the wildlife was on adrenaline in that storm.

We pulled into a convenience store in Upton. We were stuck fast, and we didn't know what to do. So we asked for help, just as the boys had done earlier that morning. The attendant engaged us with knowledge of the area and its weather. She also offered us a comfortable spot in the back room to wait out the storm.

After several hours of waiting, we discovered that a motel a quarter mile away had a vacancy, so we checked in for the night after the storm subsided. Supper at a nearby diner was satisfying. A local man, retired from Special Forces in the US military, entertained us with stories and then bought us dessert—a sweet way to end our rain-shortened day. We were grateful that others had surrounded us with counsel and encouragement.

If you do any touring by bicycle, you'll become accustomed to asking for help. It's part of the routine. When you think about it, the same is true for life itself. We simply need to exercise the humility to admit it's time to ask.

Don't be afraid to ask for help when you need it. Allowing others to help you will enhance your life—and maybe even theirs. They may have something to offer you that you don't have. After all, everyone has special gifts and a unique perspective. If you've hit a complete standstill, it's a sign you need help. Take the opportunity to jump-start your life by tapping into the people around you.

....

Where there is no counsel, the people fall;
but in the multitude of counselors there is safety.

PROVERBS 11:14

....

Personal REFLECTION:

1. When was the last time you asked someone for advice? Did it help?

2. Would you rather solicit advice while you still have the ability to solve your own problems or only when you're desperate?

3. How would you feel if a relative or a friend didn't ask for assistance from you on a problem with which he or she needed direction, even though that person knew you could help?

LESSON 31

Unexpected Stop

When setbacks come, don't assume they spell the end
of your journey. They may simply be a special provision
to support the remainder of your trek.

BY TIM

Sometimes, life throws us a curveball. The unexpected has the
power to thwart, frustrate, and alter our course. It breeds wherever
plans and real life intersect. When Debbie and I were headed
toward New Hampshire and, ultimately, the Mom-to-Mom Tour's final
destination of Houlton, Maine—and with less than four hundred miles
remaining—a surprise interrupted our plans.

As we crossed over I-90 in Upton, Massachusetts, the beautiful
greenery surrounding the highway took a backseat to the hubbub it
tolerates: the incessant whirr of rubber on asphalt, the revving of tractor-
trailer engines, and the honking horns of irate motorists competing for
lane space on the congested highway. The tumult of the interstate was a
stark reminder of our everyday life at home in Massachusetts. That was
the last place we wanted to be, because we hadn't completed our tour yet.

Soon, we were cycling through tree-shrouded back roads, with their blind ups and downs, twists and turns. We had only escaped the traffic fray temporarily when Route 9 appeared several miles later. We found ourselves right in the midst of the commotion. Once the traffic light turned green, we crossed the busy four-lane road along with the pile of cars lined up beside us. We were not ready to return to more of that!

Interstate 90, Upton, Massachusetts

Debbie had been in some discomfort with intestinal cramps for a few days. The cramps had become more than an ignorable inconvenience. My wife is tough. Otherwise, she would not have survived our first coast-to-coast trek or the weeks of cycling in mid 90-degree heat and humidity earlier in the Mom-to-Mom Tour. She excels at physical activities requiring strength and stamina, and doesn't let much of anything stop her. Yet the cramping was not going away. It had begun to hamper her and slow our progress.

Changing course with roughly a week left in our tour and Debbie's return to school looming would be difficult, particularly for two task-driven people. However, we squeezed the handlebars and jerked them toward Marlborough, where we lived, deciding to divert for a day or so, pending a medical opinion. Stopping then wasn't easy, but it was the right move. Our nearby home would provide an excellent outpost to regroup for the final push to our destination.

The doctor deemed Debbie's condition not serious, thank goodness. Nevertheless, we would need some time to rest. We watched the clock as we caught up on other matters, hopeful that Debbie would feel well enough to resume our Mom-to-Mom Tour in the next day or two.

A curveball is one view of what stopped our progress; God's provision for safety is another. How was it we had cycled without incident for over two thousand miles in more oppressive conditions than the prior few days? As our bicycle route deposited us a mere few miles from our home and from services that could help us complete our journey, our instinct to seek medical attention overrode other goals. We were glad the discomfort occurred when it did as opposed to earlier. We couldn't have arranged the scenario better had we been able to control it.

The exquisite timing of our stop reminded me of a fresh accident scene we had ridden through a day earlier in Connecticut. The accident appeared serious. Had we not taken a break a few miles beforehand, would we have arrived at the accident scene at the worst possible moment, only to become part of it? Conventional wisdom says, "Timing is everything." We are thankful our destiny lies in the hands of the One who created time.

When you find yourself paused at a stop not of your own choosing, you can get upset or you can take advantage of the opportunity to equip yourself for the next phase of your journey. Perhaps there's a reason you're sidelined. If you set aside your impatience, frustration, or anger, you'll be in a better frame of mind to consider your next steps once your traffic light turns green. You can be thankful for the diversion, because you might not make it to your next stop—or to your ultimate destination—without it.

It is not for you to know times or seasons which the Father has put in His own authority.

ACTS 1:7

Personal REFLECTION:

1. Do you view a diversion from your progress toward a goal as a provision to help you achieve it or as an unfortunate roadblock?

2. Think of the last time you were diverted from pursuing a goal. Did you achieve the goal anyway? If not, did the diversion benefit you—or someone else—more than if you'd achieved your goal?

3. Have you ever considered that what appears as a problem or inconvenience could really be God at work answering a prayer in an unexpected way?

LESSON 32

Healing Power

When you experience a miracle, it's time to let others
know about it.

BY DEBBIE

I have been amazed by the healing power of God. When I asked
God to take away my bulimia back in early summer 1986, I
stopped bingeing and purging six months later. In 1988, a few
days before my birthday in November, I went to my first AA meeting,
and I "got sober" in June of 1989. God hears our cry for help and
healing.

Sometimes, we are healed instantly, and sometimes, it takes
time. Since I became a Christian, I have had to wait a long time for
some prayers to be answered. Throughout my thirties and forties, I
prayed for a husband. Tim and I did not get married until we were
both fifty-two.

When we stopped bicycling for two weeks in the middle of
TheHopeLine Tour due to severe pain in my right leg, I prayed for

the pain to go away, for an accurate diagnosis, and for us to be able to finish our bike trip. I asked so many people to pray for my leg. My small group at our church, my mom, my friends, and people at churches we visited in Vermillion, South Dakota, and Sioux City, Iowa, all said they were praying for my leg.

For the fifteen days we stayed in Sioux City, my leg wasn't getting much better. In fact, I was looking into ways to get home. I thought that any more serious bicycling on that trip would be a lost cause and that I would need at least a month or two away from any exercise.

Tim and I are not quitters, though. We kept praying, and three days before we actually left, we thought we might be able to leave on the following day, a Saturday, to test my leg. The forecast was for gorgeous weather, but Tim noticed severe weather was expected Sunday, so we agreed to depart on Monday. We would ride south to Council Bluffs in two days and then consider how to get home from there if my leg could not handle the mileage ahead. On Saturday, we went out on a fifteen-mile test run in Sioux City. When we came back, my leg did not feel roadworthy.

When we headed out on Monday, we were cautiously hopeful that I could ride without much discomfort. Was the bat that clung to my foot before departure an omen for us to stay put? *No!*

In my first two days after returning to the road, I felt better than I had felt on the entire trip. The message I "heard" from the Lord in Sioux City was, "Embrace rest!" Even though the leg didn't feel much better during our stay, those two weeks were healing times. I slept, I rested, and I slowed down—probably for the first time in years. And when we finally hit the road, I had no pain after forty miles. On the following day, after sixty-seven miles, I was still pain free. I'd experienced a miraculous healing!

During our stay in Sioux City, a portion of Hebrews 12:1 kept running through my head: *"and let us run with endurance the race that is set before us."* I guess I would replace *run* with *bike*. It seems

God wants us to finish what we start. He won't love us any more if we finish or any less if we don't. But if He calls us to do something, He will empower us to complete it. Lord willing, we planned to bicycle much farther, one pedal stroke at a time, on TheHopeLine Tour. For me, those pedal strokes would be without pain, thanks to a miraculous healing in the Midwest!

Back on the road again in Iowa

One thing I know: that though I was blind, now I see.

JOHN 9:25B

Personal REFLECTION:

1. When was the last time you had something unusual and unexplainable happen to you or someone in your life, resulting in some sort of blessing?

2. Were you concerned about what people might think of you if you told them about it?

3. How will you react the next time something miraculous happens in your life? Will you give credit to God or simply chalk it up to good fortune?

SECTION

V

Riding through Storms

No one's journey through life comes without resistance and setbacks. Discouragement is one thing, but getting knocked clear off your feet is quite another.

You might have had to backtrack, and now you're faced with covering the same ground all over again. Perhaps you've encountered such strong opposition that you can't make progress no matter how hard you try. Other times, you may simply have taken the wrong road and found yourself off course. Sometimes, relationships cause difficulties. Perhaps a relationship that you hoped would add joy to your journey has made things much more trying instead.

Learning how to adapt to resistance and how to cooperate with others can bring deeper joy, contentment, and fulfillment to your travels. Your difficulties are a temporary time of testing. The sun will shine again on the other side of your storms.

SECTION V TAKEAWAYS
Things to Help Me Persevere

1.

2.

3.

4.

5.

LESSON 33

Meeting with Resistance

Be prepared for resistance because it's inevitable. Once
you've learned to adapt, you'll come out the other side
better for it.

BY DEBBIE

Anyone who has ever been on the plains of South Dakota knows it's windy there. Tim and I had never bicycled in South Dakota until TheHopeLine Tour, so we didn't realize how difficult the wind could be—until day forty-three of our tour. We tackled a huge hill after leaving our rustic cabin on the Missouri River in the morning. Yet the climb paled in comparison to the unrelenting wind we encountered as we headed south and east from the Snake Creek Recreational Area.

Give me hills over a headwind any day! I love tailwinds. They push me farther and faster than I would have thought possible. However, with a headwind, even when I want to move, I can't. Wind can be a humbling foe or a good friend, depending on which direction it is blowing.

At times that day, we were on flat terrain, and I was pushing to go merely six miles per hour. In my twenties and thirties, I could run faster than that. Even when we rode downhill, we could only muster ten miles per hour. Normally, a downhill ride might get us up to forty miles per hour. Cycling into the wind that day was a struggle, as it took us over five hours to go only forty-four miles.

Climbing from the banks of the Missouri River in South Dakota

We stopped in Bonesteel for a break from the wind and to decide what our journey forward should be for the remainder of the day. Many of the towns we bicycled through on the Adventure Cycling maps had either one motel or none. Bonesteel happened to have a small motel run by a ninety-year-old woman named Marge. According to the sign, Marge did not take credit cards, and rooms went for thirty dollars a night.

Outside the motel, we met a pair of sisters who were visiting their ninety-eight-year-old mother (who was a friend of Marge). I hit it off with them right away. They highly recommended the motel. Marge, however, was out of town and wouldn't be back until later, so Tim and I hung out talking to the sisters and getting some insight into the town of Bonesteel. It seemed everyone in that town was related somehow.

The most enjoyable part of traveling through South Dakota was the small, friendly communities. People would look us in the eye and greet us with a hello or a wave. They seemed contented and relaxed, enjoying everyday life. I found the slower pace of life refreshing. Maybe the wind had slowed them down too. It sure had done that to us. It's a good thing, because otherwise we would have missed the friendly ambiance.

The South Dakotans I talked with accepted the wind as part of everyday life. Maybe I needed to do the same, even though it was knocking me back with every turn of my pedals. Fighting the breeze simply wasn't working. I couldn't change its direction, so why fight it or complain about it?

Such is the case with life. When you meet with resistance, it's important to adjust your expectations and your pace. Maybe it's time for a break, to enjoy what you missed while you struggled to move forward, and to allow time for the circumstances to change in your favor. You can wrestle with your uncontrollable circumstances and wear yourself out with little to show for it, or you can accept them and make the most of your situation. Regardless, difficulties will make you stronger for the road ahead.

When you meet resistance and adjust your pace accordingly, you preserve your energy for times when your efforts will be more fruitful. It's helpful to recognize which things you can change and which you can't. Accepting what you can't change and working to change what you can will maximize your progress.

My brethren, count it all joy when you fall into various trials, knowing that the testing of your faith produces patience. But let patience have its perfect work, that you may be perfect and complete, lacking nothing.

JAMES 1:2-4

Personal REFLECTION:

1. Are you facing a gentle headwind that will make you stronger, or are you spending all of your energy fighting a gale without getting anywhere?

2. What circumstance in your life is your strongest wind of resistance? Are you willing to wait for the wind to shift in your favor?

3. How do you decide whether to wait for a wind of resistance to change direction or to proceed through it at a slower pace?

LESSON 34

Rough Riding

When the riding gets rough, don't lose sight of the big
picture. Difficult circumstances are usually temporary.
You'll find relief on the other side and have a better
appreciation for the blessings in life.

BY DEBBIE

Not all roads are created equal, especially when you are on two
tires with no shock absorbers. Since we'd left Missoula on
TheHopeLine Tour, we'd cobbled together our own trail, but
it wasn't always smooth.

A conversation I overheard at breakfast in Livingston, Montana, five
days later made me glad we had chosen not to go through Yellowstone
National Park, as our bicycling maps would have directed us. A man who
had driven through Yellowstone mentioned that a bicyclist was run off
the road and suffered severe road rash. We were also far away from a mad
crowd of tourists, who no doubt were huddled in the abutting corners of
Montana and Wyoming awaiting their next bear sighting. Even so, the
route ahead of us on that day came with its own issues.

We should have known the name "Convict Grade Road" might
indicate some kind of challenge. We were warned that fugitives hide

from the law in Montana, but that road was hiding something else: pavement!

We started out on it splendidly, with no traffic and wonderful scenery. About a mile or two down the road, however, we found ourselves riding on gravel for not one or two miles but twenty. Another road had started out pleasantly, enticing us with the same misleading façade, only to turn on us once we had taken the bait. Neither the map nor any signage steered us clear of this slow and, at times, treacherous form of travel.

Google Maps for bicycles must be for mountain bikes. We needed to concentrate without interruption to balance our bikes on those bumpy and slippery gravel roads and to make any headway on them. Gaining traction in the loose gravel was a seemingly endless pursuit. When I did take my eyes off the road, however, I saw more of the gorgeous scenery that characterizes Montana.

We entered the short-grass prairie region and cycled alongside some deer several times, as well as bulls and horses. We even sighted some predatory birds we thought might be eagles. One of my lessons on that day was to remember the big picture in life. Don't simply focus on the dirt and gravel in the immediate line of sight. Look up periodically to see the beauty all around, even if it means taking a break.

Toward the end of the day, we hopped onto I-90 for several miles out of necessity, since the frontage road stopped there. After riding on gravel roads for so long, a portion of interstate travel was welcome relief. Tim couldn't tell from the map where the frontage road resumed, so we exited the interstate to investigate. No one was around except for a couple standing out in a field, with their car parked nearby. We beckoned to them, and they came over to talk with us.

They warned us of the upcoming construction on I-90 and the two-way traffic we would encounter on the bridge that crosses the Yellowstone River. The eastbound bridge was under repair and impassable, even by bicycle. They offered to help us across the dangerous stretch. We accepted their proposal gladly and headed toward the highway with a head start.

We arrived at the temporary traffic light that regulated the flow of traffic across the open "westbound" bridge and waited there for our new friends. As their vehicle approached, they signaled for us to go. Moments later, however, a barreling tractor-trailer prevented them from slowing down, and they passed us by, as did the tractor-trailer and many other vehicles.

Soon, the traffic light changed, even though we'd only cycled one-quarter of the way across the bridge. Almost immediately, a steady stream of high-speed, westbound traffic met us. We continued on, balancing our wide and heavy loads on the three-foot shoulder while oncoming tractor-trailers sped by. There was no place to stop to wait for the traffic light's next cycle. Regardless, we rode through safely.

When we exited the interstate several miles later, we noticed our travel advisors had stopped on the next frontage road to check on us. Soon, we met them there.

They handed each of us a bottle of water, and we chatted at length. Talking to another woman encouraged me. Our bike adventure inspired her. She said she wanted to get back into exercising. Meanwhile, Tim was discussing TheHopeLine with her husband. We discovered these two individuals were fellow believers, which seemed too coincidental. We had that same feeling of camaraderie we have whenever we spend time with like-minded folks. The encounter provided a smooth transition from some considerably rough riding.

A relatively easy ride into Columbus allowed us to enjoy pleasurable views over the Yellowstone River at sunset. We'd been challenged on that day with some difficulties, yet total strangers had comforted us along the way. We would continue after a rest day to more spellbinding views and smooth travel as we relished our remaining miles in Montana. What a beautiful state, filled with spectacular scenery!

Whenever you encounter a rough patch in life, it seems there's always relief on the other side. But if you don't resolve to push through the challenges, you won't enjoy the refreshment that awaits you. The troubles won't stay with you forever. Eventually, they'll leave you with a more balanced perspective. You'll find that the high points down the road will take on even greater significance as past troubles fade into the background.

. . . .

For our light affliction, which is but for a moment, is working for us a far more exceeding and eternal weight of glory.

2 CORINTHIANS 4:17

. . . .

Personal REFLECTION:

1. Think of a time when you faced a monumental difficulty. How did you react? When things improved, how did you feel?

2. If you're in the middle of trouble right now, recall how things were when life was easier. Hang on and be encouraged, because you will likely return there soon.

3. What does having a balanced perspective mean to you? Do you have one?

LESSON 35

Held Back

As we pursue our goals, we'll meet another type of resistance, one not born of natural phenomena, yet its presence is as palpable as that of its physical counterparts. It abides in areas beset with troubles and in people who choose to live addicted to perpetual misery, complete with attitudes to match.

BY TIM

O n day thirty-four of the Mom-to-Mom Tour, we crossed the Delaware River from New Jersey and arrived in Easton, Pennsylvania, on Saturday evening at dusk.

The light of Sunday morning revealed more about our surroundings. After walking the streets for an hour looking for churches, we were disappointed in our two options. Both appeared closed. An inquiry at a local eatery substantiated our discussion at the front desk of our motel the prior evening: church was not a priority there.

Finally, we discovered another church, a long-standing institution whose attendees had plenty of gray hair but who lacked the vitality of youth in their midst. Furthermore, their dwindling numbers suggested their large, aging facility would go the way of its counterparts. They were well-meaning people committed in their beliefs, but their traditional church was not pulling in new blood.

Outside the motel after church, a local warned of a troubled area where drug abuse and prostitution abounded. We hadn't seen overt evidence of this on our prior evening's stroll to a pizza shop, but we had sensed that not all was well in this area.

On our hurried ride through a town across the river the previous day, we had seen a similar scene. It lacked cleanliness, well-maintained buildings, and industriousness, and it seemed impoverished. People with surly looks on their faces were hanging out with seemingly too much time on their hands, smoking and bickering with family and friends. By all appearances, life was not what it had been in yesteryear, not what one might like to live in, and certainly not what one might hope for their children's future. Closed businesses and factories along the river heading north suggested even harder times ahead.

With beautiful surroundings merely a mile or two outside of town, couldn't the townsfolk break free from these circumstances to enjoy the scenery? Yet these rural areas were ours for the taking, with no kindred spirits in sight. I couldn't help but wonder whether a community adrift from God helped explain the conditions. Although honoring God may not be the popular concept it once was, it still seemed a fair and appropriate question to ponder.

Scenery along the Delaware River

After our late start due to church and bicycle maintenance, and still feeling the effects of eighty-seven miles in the saddle the day before, we traveled slower. The weather was ideal for cycling. We enjoyed the New Jersey side of the Delaware Water Gap National Recreational Area before crossing back to Pennsylvania, where steeper hills and more traffic slowed us down even more.

We stopped in the borough of Delaware Water Gap, Pennsylvania, to eat. A review of the map and the clock suggested we lacked sufficient time to reach a motel before sundown, despite several more hours of gorgeous daylight remaining. We were tired and listless, so we decided to stay in town to rest up for the next day.

Somehow, the low mileage for the day and our own lethargy reflected the ambiance of that day's launching point. Could a spiritual malaise have rubbed off on us or at least aimed to drag us down as we sought to escape it?

You can't divorce yourself from your immediate setting. Your mood and behavior are susceptible to its influence. When you travel through life, you'll pass through dark patches before you even realize what hit you. They can't penetrate well-clad spiritual armor, but they can make your pathway difficult and bog down your progress as if you were treading through quicksand. Keep your senses attuned for these trouble spots. Unless you feel called as a missionary to such settings, proceed toward the nearest exit as swiftly as possible. You can spread good cheer on your way out the door, but make sure you don't overstay your welcome.

The same caution applies to dealing with difficult people who bring you the oppression of their chosen misery. You can love people and share the truth with them, but you can't help people who don't want to be helped, nor can you change the way they feel and behave. They may even resent you for trying. If they're an inescapable part of your life, love them the best way you know how. Figuring out just how to do that will likely require some prayer and soul-searching.

· ·

For we do not wrestle against flesh and blood, but against principalities, against powers, against the rulers of the darkness of this age, against spiritual hosts of wickedness in the heavenly places.

EPHESIANS 6:12

· ·

Personal REFLECTION:

1. Do you believe there are forces of spiritual darkness that can thwart you? If so, what can you do to combat them?

2. Who constantly drags you down?

3. Have you leveled with the difficult people in your life and challenged them to grow? What boundaries can you establish with them to avoid becoming a victim of their unhappiness?

LESSON 36

Hells Canyon

It pays to consider now, before it is too late,
what will happen to you after you die.

BY TIM

We should have known we'd run into opposition when we embarked on TheHopeLine Tour to promote hope. Maybe we should have paid more attention to the names of the places on the route we'd selected—particularly the area we encountered on day fourteen. Our overnight neighbor at the Copperfield Campground on the Snake River in Oxbow, Oregon, had coached us about the need to ride early in the morning there. They don't call that place "Hells Canyon" for nothing. An early start would allow us to climb out of the oppressive valley heat and make our way into Idaho.

However, after seventy miles in a scorcher the day before—and with our propensity to fumble through a camping experience as novices—not surprisingly, we started out that morning later than we should have. Keeping up with bicycle touring chores while at a campground is not one of our strengths. In addition, our fifty-six-year-old bodies—lying on air mattresses stuffed into a small tent—hadn't rested as well as they might have years earlier.

We slipped even further behind schedule a few miles along the Oregon side of the Snake River when we met a bicycling couple from Scotland traveling in the opposite direction. They were about to put the final revolutions on their trip across America on the TransAmerica Trail. With nearly four thousand miles behind them, they had many stories and impressions to share as the forenoon temperature continued its ascent. Finally, we parted ways and proceeded to Brownlee Dam, where we crossed over the Snake River into Idaho. We were only ten miles into our day, but at least we had entered our second state on TheHopeLine Tour.

The road on the Idaho side of the river came with some twists and turns. Portions of the road hung perilously close to the cliff along the reservoir. Engineers had clearly understood this when they erected a chain-link fence to save those who might veer too close to the edge. Nevertheless, the precipice intimidated us enough to push us into the middle of the road. We kept a close watch ahead and behind for vehicles that might further challenge our high-wire act.

Climbing out of Hells Canyon in Idaho

As midday approached, the heat index was climbing faster than we were. Debbie's portable thermometer registered 100 degrees, and it would head higher before the end of our climb.

We left the river behind and began a much steeper ascent out of the abyss. Given the area's name, the phrase "hotter than hell" came to mind.

These deep canyons of the high western desert are interesting phenomena. We'd been on the other end of Hells Canyon on our first tour. True to its name, the lower you go, the hotter it gets.

Where did such phraseology originate? No one has ever been to hell with a thermometer in hand, near as I can tell. If they have, they've not been back to report on it. "Hotter than hell" wouldn't exist without ancient writings passed down over the years, including those recorded in the Bible. Other than as a cuss word, hell isn't a very popular topic in this era of political correctness, even within the church. Yet it seems foolhardy to ignore something so important.

The Bible describes hell as a lake of fire where sinners will burn for the evil things they've done. Further consideration of Scripture suggests we'll all end up there if we haven't asked God to forgive our sins. Some of us may have more sins to our detriment than others do, but we all have them. Failing to live up to the perfect standard puts all of us in the same boat—the one chartered for the lake of fire. If you believe what the Bible says, only Jesus can rescue us from that sinking ship.

Thinking about hell reminded me of an encounter we'd had the day before at the Shorthorn Bar and Grill in Richland, Oregon. We'd met a short, stocky fellow there who had bicycled from Los Angeles on a recumbent bike and was heading east, as we were. He was an experienced bicycle tourist—and an experienced man, with gray hair standing on end, framing his balding head. The weathered look on his square face, which was half-covered by a pair of large, equally square wire-rimmed eyeglasses, seemed more a result of life than the sun or the wind. We met him while engaging another solo cross-country cyclist named Michael, a twenty-six-year-old video producer from New York City. Michael had made his lonely way across most of the country. He described unrelenting headwinds in Kansas, where locals rescued him from tornadoes. Later, mechanical problems with his bicycle dogged him in Colorado. He was more than ready to finish, which we found hard to imagine. Why would anyone want to end a long-distance bicycle tour and return to ordinary life?

The loud, gray-haired man was letting the whole restaurant know about the religious group down at the campground where he'd stayed the previous evening. Apparently, the experience had led to a sleepless night and fueled his disdain for organized religion. Later, we saw and spoke with several conservatively clad, bearded men riding older bicycles down Main Street. They were into a simpler life and seemed pleasant enough. Yet the man from LA seemed agitated and began badmouthing them and their beliefs. His words and intonations spewed venom at anyone in the restaurant who might have had some love and respect for God. Debbie and I consider ourselves part of that group.

"I'm going to hell," he proclaimed. Then, he laughed fiendishly.

He continued on, mocking the claims of Christianity, punctuating each sentence with devilish and overbearing laughter. He had plenty to share while showing little respect for conventional religious teaching.

Finally, I decided to interrupt him. Heretofore, I could have been in his camp, for all he knew. However, his one-way discourse needed more balance, and I thought it might be helpful if he considered an important question. I never want to "beat people over the head with the Bible," but I do want them to know what it says about what might happen to them when they die. I also want them to understand their options, if they don't already.

"You seem very sure of yourself," I said. "You're laughing at the notion you might go to hell when you die. Doesn't that concern you? What if hell is real, and what if the Bible is true?"

My query shifted his sarcasm into a higher gear. His arrogant laughter increased, as did his volume. His defense seemed well rehearsed, although a bit nonsensical, without leaving any pauses for rebuttal. He dropped scientist Carl Sagan's name for added effect.

Debbie had about had it with his obnoxious attitude and his grating laughter. I simply let him go on. No response was necessary, nor could I think of one suitable as a follow-up. I like to respect people's perspectives and their right to choose what they believe. I'm open to presenting God's case as best I can, but I'm not inclined to argue it, especially when there appears to be no genuine interest. I think healthy discussions based on historical events, time-tested teachings, and personal experience can be helpful to sincere seekers. Nothing I heard from this man suggested he was in that category.

During all of this, Michael sat quietly in the corner finishing lunch, perhaps wondering, like we were, what was behind this or how he could extricate himself from the situation. Maybe, deep down, he was enjoying it while regretting having no video camera in hand to record the show.

Soon, Debbie and I paid our bill and left. Sometimes, having to move on to the next stop on a bicycle tour has its advantages.

"What do you suppose happened to him to make him so angry and close-minded to spiritual matters?" I asked Debbie.

I couldn't help but feel sorry for him. Maybe he'd lost a parent in childhood, gone through a nasty divorce, or suffered some trauma in the military. Perhaps hypocrites in a local church had turned on him. Regardless, we had just witnessed a sad and sorry outburst from a troubled man. I wished we could have helped him somehow.

Meanwhile, the steep climb out of the heat continued. Escaping the clutches of Hells Canyon was not easy. The heat was more intense due to the early-afternoon sun. With sweat dripping from us like water from a leaky water bottle, we continued crawling up the hill with our heavy loads until an oasis appeared in the form of a store with accompanying lunch counter. A driveway two hundred feet wide separated the store from the road. Rather than push our loads across the gravel, we chose to drop them roadside and trudge toward the store without them.

We entered the air-conditioned eatery and ordered lunch. While we were waiting, who do you suppose walked in but the angry man we'd met the day before! I suppose when you are making your way out of Hells Canyon, you should expect an opposing spirit would chase you. Even the name of the river that cut the canyon bears the serpent's name.

Clearly parched, the spent man approached the counter clamoring for water. Pushing a fully loaded recumbent bicycle out of that canyon in 100-degree heat would surely stress anyone's system. He sat down at a table across the way with the same agitation and restlessness we had detected the day before. A quick glance our way resulted in no conversation between us. He looked like he had no more energy for it.

Debbie and I made it out of Hells Canyon alive, despite my light-headedness and a twenty-minute restroom break dealing with severe cramps at a convenience store in Cambridge. The brutal climb in the stifling heat had really gotten to me. Forty miles was enough for that day.

We will always remember the man we encountered as we traveled in and out of Hells Canyon, but not with the same fondness we have for many others we've met on the road. After leaving the abyss behind, we never saw him again. I wonder what might have become of him on his trip across America, but more importantly, on his journey through life. He did not seem destined for a good place, and we feared for his safety. He would ride his recumbent bicycle alone through all kinds of hazardous weather while barreling tractor-trailers, grizzly bears, and aggressive dogs watched on. We hope he had a successful ride and time to reconsider his long-term options.

> **And anyone not found written in the Book of Life was cast into the lake of fire.**
> REVELATION 20:15

Personal REFLECTION:

1. Have you ever met a person like the man in the story? What was your reaction?

2. Do you believe there is a place called hell? If so, how does one avoid it?

3. If you die tomorrow, do you know where you will go?

LESSON 37

His Needs, Her Needs

Sometimes, your challenges will be relational. When
those challenges arise in marriage, it's critically important
to address them and make adjustments. A marriage
gone awry will affect all other facets of life.

BY DEBBIE

When you begin a bicycle tour with your spouse, how you relate to each other changes. You're no longer in the routine of everyday life. And although you're with one another all the time, you're still alone on your bicycle with plenty of time to think. A week into TheHopeLine Tour, the prior Sunday's sermon had me thinking about relationships and the love part of the tagline for our Open Road Press website, which is "Love and Life by Bicycle."

Several days earlier while riding, I had been thinking of three words to describe Tim. It didn't take too long to come up with "smart," "kind," and "patient." At dinner that night, I asked him to describe me in three words, and he came up with "vivacious," "energetic," and "joyful." He added that I am not joyful all the time—not too many people are—but it was music to my ears to hear his descriptors. Most women I know love to hear words of affirmation. Men need them too.

Contemplating love

At TheHopeLine, the first two things we do as Hope Coaches when interacting with young people are listen to them and encourage them. Both of these verbs help build relationships. They work well with a spouse, a friend, or a stranger. We all need to be heard and encouraged daily.

At church the previous Sunday, the pastor started a series entitled "His Needs, Her Needs" based on a book with the same title by Willard Harley. Do you know the five needs of men and women? Maybe you've figured them out on your own, but in case you're wondering, here's what the pastor said:

Men's Needs	Women's Needs
SEXUAL FULFILLMENT	AFFECTION
AN ATTRACTIVE SPOUSE	CONVERSATION
A RECREATIONAL COMPANION	HONESTY AND OPENNESS
DOMESTIC SUPPORT	FINANCIAL SUPPORT
ADMIRATION	FAMILY COMMITMENT

I've definitely accumulated some points as Tim's recreational companion on our bicycle tours! I love riding with him, even if my need for conversation goes unmet. Carrying on a conversation while bicycling is nearly impossible. Thank goodness we have plenty of time off the bike for the other needs on the lists.

Recognizing that men and women are wired differently helps us understand each other better. Yet the wiring can make things difficult, because we have some contrasting needs. We think differently, and that can make it hard to communicate or to agree on something. Even so, those very differences enrich our lives as we journey together, because we complement one another. We wouldn't fit together as well if we each had the same qualities, needs, and desires. Our differences expand us and help make us into the people God wants us to be.

Everyone will have relational challenges, because, as people, we are inherently self-centered. Inevitably, one person's desire will conflict with another's. The closer the relationship, the higher the potential for conflict. Understanding the unique needs of others, especially our spouse, will help us navigate relationships better. Considering other people's needs unlocks potential blessings on our trek through life.

So God created man in His own image; in the image of God He created him; male and female He created them.

GENESIS 1:27

Personal REFLECTION:

1. The next time you converse with someone, listen to what the other person is saying and acknowledge the message by repeating it back to him or her. Consider adding some encouraging words to strengthen the relationship.

2. Are there some recurring issues with your spouse or a special friend that you should try to resolve now before they escalate? Consider discussing it with him or her.

3. If you can't resolve your differences by talking through them, can you think of a third party you can call upon for help?

LESSON 38

Major Meltdown

The stress of pursuing goals sometimes can lead to
relational meltdowns. If you're not willing or able to make
adjustments, you're sure to run aground.

BY DEBBIE

I thought that being more mature as a newlywed would be an advantage, since younger couples have less life experience. Tim and I had satisfying single lives before we married. I traveled alone frequently. Our honeymoon on wheels would be a piece of cake for us, or so I thought. We would bike and talk, spend romantic evenings together, and make up for all those lonely nights when we were not married. That was my vision when we left Seaside, Oregon, on our first bike tour.

Never did I suspect we would be in conflict so early in the journey. I remember my shock when the staff at the bike shop in Maine said many marriages break up when couples bicycle across the country. The unrelenting togetherness is too much for some to handle. I scoffed at those comments. Little did I know I would feel disgruntled with Tim in less than three weeks of marriage!

Before embarking, I had spoken to one of my best friends in Colorado about a cross-country tour. She had completed one with her husband several years earlier. She said it was one of the best experiences of her life, rated almost as high as her wedding and the birth of her daughter. She spoke of the laughter and camaraderie she and her husband had shared. I had high expectations of bonding with Tim on our bike trip and setting the stage for a lifetime of connectedness and marital bliss.

We were clueless about the amount of time, energy, and work it would take to bicycle across the country. Neither of us were experienced campers, so even setting up camp was a major ordeal. Add a flat tire at dusk, signs warning of rattlesnakes at our first campsite in Crow Butte, Washington, and unrealistic expectations of romantic love, and you have the perfect formula for a meltdown. That's where I was headed.

The daytime heat of the high desert was also taking its toll. Granted, it was dry, but I was still uncomfortable riding in 95-degree heat. One thing I did hope for on that trip was to get going early each day. That was a strong recommendation from my Colorado friend: *"Beat the heat and ride early."* Tim likes to burn the midnight oil, which hindered early-morning riding and caused conflict between us from the start. Starting out at one thirty in the afternoon the next day curdled my steaming milk of a mood. By the time we stopped at a convenience store and restaurant in Paterson, the sun had become so hot, we were parched. We couldn't escape the heat soon enough. I truly wanted to end the trip, but I knew in my heart of hearts I could not.

After our break, we continued to ride with simmering anger and arrived at our hotel barely talking. During one stop, I had been very disrespectful to Tim, and he'd responded, "I am your husband now, and you need to show me some respect." As much as his statement made me feel like a naughty child, I knew it was true. We belonged to each other since marrying, and I wanted to be a wife who honored her husband with respect, just as Tim was trying to show me that he'd love me no matter what.

At dinner that night in Umatilla, Oregon, we sat in stone silence. In my years of waitressing, I remember couples like us that night. I also recognized one of my biggest fears: married and going out to dinner with anger as an appetizer and nothing to say for the main course. Our steak knives proved inadequate to cut the tension, nor could our napkins clean up the discord.

We went back to our room, videoconferenced Tim's mom, and tried to put on a happy face. After we signed off, we knew it was time to deal with our conflict. We hadn't married to be miserable. There we were with a fantastic opportunity to cycle across America. But without togetherness, we wouldn't enjoy it or maybe even make it home safely.

Our prayer time was an effective way to reconcile. We use it to this day. We have an all-knowing Arbiter who loves us unconditionally and has a plan for our union. He doubles as our Advocate. When we come to Him in prayer, I am able to say things to Him that Tim can hear (and vice versa), including expressing my anger, hurt, frustration, and disappointment. Each of us so respects our gracious Arbiter that we simply listen to what our mate says rather than lashing out at each other, as we'd done beforehand. Even if we can't express those emotions, we can at least agree on other matters in prayer. Then, our masterful Arbiter softens our hearts, quells the internal uprising, and pulls us back together. Oftentimes, the Scripture we've read beforehand can act as a stimulus to reform our attitudes. Then, we are able to speak to one another more civilly and begin to acknowledge one another. Finally, our Advocate uses the practical benefits of a good night's sleep to restore us for another day. I'm grateful for this formula.

We expect to have conflicts, but they don't have to lead to meltdowns. My black or white thinking gets me in trouble sometimes, such as on that day in Umatilla. I did not need to end the trip permanently by flying back to Massachusetts and letting Tim finish on his own. Nor did I have to suffer in silence and not tell him what was upsetting me. I had to live in the "gray area" and realize that some days are better than others.

I've learned that it takes time and patience for a newly married couple to bond. When you encounter conflict with your spouse, rather than going on the offensive, check your expectations to make sure they are reasonable. Try to see things from your partner's point of view. Usually, when you reach out to meet your mate halfway, you'll discover that he or she will come your way, too.

When you marry someone, you're in it for the long haul. Many miles remain in your trip, and you need one another to complete it. Be willing to consider what you can do to make it work. Otherwise, you'll not be very happy going it alone.

> **Therefore a man shall leave his father and mother and be joined to his wife, and they shall become one flesh.**
>
> GENESIS 2:24

Personal REFLECTION:

1. When you had your last major meltdown with your spouse or, if you're single, a friend, were you able to resolve it? How?

2. Would you rather pursue peace or get your own way?

3. What issue causes you the most conflict with your spouse or close friends? Think about your expectations surrounding this issue and ask a trusted third party if he or she thinks your expectations are reasonable. Ask your spouse or friends to do the same.

LESSON 39

Adventuresome Spirit

When you travel through life with someone else, nurturing his or her unique character attributes will enhance your own life. On the other hand, not allowing room for them will slow the journey and bring about some rough riding.

By Tim

Debbie and I don't always see eye to eye. We tend to approach things differently. Never was that more apparent than on day thirty-eight of our honeymoon on wheels.

We were at a motel in Wilton, Iowa. When I walked outside at nine thirty in the morning and saw the ominous sky, it spooked me. I heard rumbling in the distance. I went back into the room to pay closer attention to The Weather Channel, which had serenaded us as we dressed. We'd heard this tune before, but never so loud in our immediate surroundings. When the weathercasters mentioned the possibility of tornadoes yet again, anxiety welled up within me.

Debbie was undergoing her morning ritual, which she anticipated would end the same way it always did when we toured, with us wheeling our bicycles out of the motel room soon and pedaling away to another day's adventure. However, I wasn't convinced it was business as usual. Her humming and upbeat spirit belied the threatening sky outside. Didn't she realize we were headed for a storm?

"Debbie, did you hear what they just said?" I asked curtly.

Before she could answer, we heard a knock on the door.

"Housekeeping. May I come in?"

We opened the door to another friendly midwesterner, who was equipped to prep the small room for its next overnight guest. We welcomed her in. Perhaps I could gather some intelligence from a local, someone who'd seen a dark sky like the one outside and might know what it really meant.

"Wow! It sure looks threatening out there," I said, hoping to prompt a weather-related comment.

"Yes, they don't call this 'tornado alley' for nothing!" she quipped.

Tornado alley? That's not what I needed to hear—or perhaps it was. And maybe, just maybe, Debbie had heard it too. It was hard to miss. After some more conversation about local weather and tornadoes in that part of Iowa, our pleasant chambermaid left.

Meanwhile, Debbie continued preparing for the day.

"We need to get in a lot of miles today while it's so flat," she said. "We'll just need to put on rain gear. After all, that's why we brought it, so we can ride in the rain."

"No way!" I said. I held the long vowel sound in each word longer than usual to make sure she got the message. "We're not leaving here until the weather clears." I felt annoyed she would jeopardize our well-being so callously. Didn't she understand the power of a tornado?

Debbie didn't receive my stiff rebuke well. She thought I was being overly cautious. What's more, I suspected that the possibility of severe weather had energized her urge to hit the road. For her, it merely added to the excitement.

Her behavior reminded me of a bicycle ride we'd had in Houlton, Maine, when visiting my mother before we married. We were caught in a heavy thunderstorm—and not just any thundershower but one of those you don't forget. If you've never experienced one of Aroostook County's tumultuous storms, the thunder is so loud that it rattles the windows in your house and jumps you out of your skin. Even furry friends run for cover in that fury. But not Debbie! As we picked up the pace to make it to shelter on that particular day, all I could hear from behind me after each lightning strike and instantaneous thunderclap—the loudest I'd ever heard—was gleeful laughter.

Eventually, we reached a compromise that morning in Iowa. We had waited long enough to see the sky begin to lighten up. Even though it was still sprinkling, I agreed to venture out, to leave our token shelter in Wilton behind and join the neighboring cornfields in their encore of "Singin' in the Rain." Debbie's joyous spirit had won out. Soon, the skies cleared, and we cycled to our hearts' content, ninety miles of contentment across the Mississippi River and into Kewanee, Illinois. A beautiful sunset, in stark contrast to the morning's gloom, spotlighted the blessing of working out our differences and traveling together as one.

That day makes me think about how much Debbie challenges my prudent—some might say overcautious—approach to life. We hadn't been simply "Singin' in the Rain," we'd been "dancin' in the rain"! Yes, a dance went on that day, and if you're in close relationship with a spouse, you know what I mean. We move one another back and forth until we can step in unison. Our collective movement is unique compared to how each of us would move on our own.

God places a husband and wife together strategically, and the spouses have complementary features. Their interests may be in common, but their personalities usually aren't. Yet when they come together, over time, they develop a collective personality and spirit that honors their Creator.

A marriage isn't a random act accomplished by overactive hormones or mere chance, at least not if God is allowed to orchestrate it. No, it's by design. And in our case, I'm the beneficiary of Debbie's adventuresome spirit. If I smother that attribute, not only have I squelched her spirit and made her unhappy, I've also minimized my own gift. The same goes for her. A middle ground somewhere in between will maximize our joy as a couple and prepare us for a stronger testimonial for the God we both love. We'll make that middle ground our destination every day that we travel together in marriage.

He created them male and female, and blessed them and called them Mankind in the day they were created.

GENESIS 5:2

Personal REFLECTION:

1. If you're not married, think about your own unique traits with which you might like to bless a spouse someday. As time passes and admirers come and go, look for someone who will honor your gifting even though he or she might not have it in common with you.

2. What are some of the unique traits of your spouse or, if you're single, a close friend?

3. Plan an activity that celebrates and honors those traits.

LESSON 40

Front-row Seat to the Amazing

Prolonged resistance places you in the best seat in the
house to watch something amazing unfold. You may
even share some time on stage!

BY DEBBIE

Within twenty-four hours, lives can change. In fact, they
can change in a second, but that was not the case for
me on one particular weekend in the Ohio River Valley
during TheHopeLine Tour.

On Saturday, I started downhill, literally. Friday night, we had stayed
in Maysville, Kentucky, and the only room available was on the second
floor. With no elevator, we grimaced at the thought of carrying our
bikes upstairs. Tim handled mine by himself, but it took both of us to
carry his upstairs.

While Tim was checking out on Saturday morning, I thought I could
carry my bike downstairs as easily as he'd brought it up. I started to roll
my bike down the back stairs. I must have awakened anyone who was
sleeping with the loud crash against the wall near the landing halfway

down. I cut my leg and bruised my ego, realizing that I was not as strong as I used to be (and apparently not as smart either).

Once I cleaned up my bleeding leg and headed to the grocery store, I realized it was a gorgeous day, and I tried to correct my foul mood and my embarrassment at doing such a stupid thing.

"How many really dumb things have I done on this trip?" I asked Tim.

"I haven't been counting," he replied ever so gently.

Now, that was a kind response. Not keeping track of one another's wrongs strengthens a loving relationship.

As the day progressed, I was feeling sorry for myself, and I was becoming sick of the scenery around me. How many corn and soybean fields can one see and still appreciate them? I was also getting sick and tired of going to the bathroom—with no bathroom in sight! Darting behind a tree or into bushes, trying to time it without a car whipping by, is more challenging than you might think. I always got nervous when people down the road said something like, "We saw you back there on the road." I always wanted to ask, "Did you see me with my bike shorts up or down?" Luckily, few people saw us more than once on that trip.

The umpteenth cornfield

Tim knew I was having a hard time and kept trying to encourage me, but I was too down to see the light at the end of the tunnel. Sometimes, I forget how difficult bicycle touring is. The majority of long-distance riders we see are male. Not too many women want to endure the physical demands.

The next day would have to be better. I remember someone saying once, "Don't quit until the miracle happens." On Saturday, I felt that it would be a miracle if we finished that bicycle tour.

That evening, on our way to our hotel in Milford, Ohio, we noticed Grace Baptist Church. Sunday school was scheduled for ten o'clock, and the worship service was at eleven. We were determined to attend after such a difficult Saturday.

Sunday morning, Pastor Tim greeted us at the door and invited us to roll our bikes into an unused classroom. Then, he escorted us into separate Bible studies. I sat in with a group of five wonderful women. As soon as I sat down, my mood brightened. I shared my passion for TheHopeLine. They listened intently and asked questions that made me proud of the work Tim and I were doing.

Encouragement really has the power to lift one's spirits. Not only did my time with these women erase the gloom, I also wanted to help them with their "Lil' Bears of Grace" ministry, which they so lovingly shared. They made stuffed bears out of polar fleece and gave them to area children faced with medical challenges. Once I arrived home, I would have a sample bear waiting for me, along with the pattern to make one. I'd be able to sew some bears and brighten children's lives.

One of the women in the group had been through a few health scares with her husband and shared a powerful truth that God had taught her: *"It is in the hardest times of our lives that we have a front-row seat to watch God do something amazing!"* I could relate to that. It had certainly been true throughout TheHopeLine Tour. Knowing that God will do something amazing every day, if we lift up our eyes and focus on Him, inspires me. Anticipating His deliverance helps describe what hope is all about. I left that group of women with a new perspective and a much fuller heart than I'd had the day before. God never ceases to amaze me!

The next time God places you in the front row, take note. The show will begin soon, and you'll have the best seat in the house.

· ·

My grace is sufficient for you, for My strength is made perfect in weakness.

2 CORINTHIANS 12:9A

· ·

Personal REFLECTION:

1. When you encounter difficult times, are you inclined to give up or to persevere?

2. Think about a time when you received some needed encouragement just in time. What did it feel like? How can you provide that same sort of encouragement to someone else?

3. Do you believe that God can meet you in your time of need? If so, how?

SECTION
VI

Enjoying the Ride

After all of the preparation and struggle that go into worthwhile pursuits, savor those special moments of affirmation and surprise blessings along the way. You'll spot them through impressions and observations of the unusual or the coincidental. Having the presence of mind to recognize and celebrate them will bring the joy and fulfillment you seek on your adventures.

Don't expect the crowning moment at journey's end to bring the ultimate satisfaction. If you wait for that moment to fulfill you, you'll have missed the entire blessing. Besides, you may never reach your destination for reasons beyond your control. If you're not feeling affirmed throughout your trip, you may be on the wrong road.

SECTION VI TAKEAWAYS
Things to Celebrate

1.

2.

3.

4.

5.

LESSON 41

Nature's Object Lessons

Receiving guidance from the lessons that surround us is
a powerful blessing when traveling through life. Seeing
those lessons helps us understand we are not alone in
our pursuits. We have an ever-present Tour Guide who
enlivens our journey and helps us avoid catastrophe.

BY DEBBIE

With plenty of time to observe and ponder on a bicycle tour, we find that nature itself speaks truth when we listen. We can't help but notice roadkill. We see it every day when we tour. Usually, I look the other way to avoid its grotesqueness, but it's nearly impossible to escape the odor and the impulse to gag. On day four of the Mom-to-Mom Tour, in the heat of central Florida, Tim and I took mental notes on what we saw.

We'd never seen a dead armadillo on our bike rides in New England. The one we saw on that day in Florida hadn't yet been flattened by traffic. It was pink in some places and gray in others. The round blob of guts, gore, and raw meat lay on its side, its eyes wide open. About a foot away from it lay a large black bird, perhaps a raven, freshly killed thanks to its desire for a roadside snack and a collision with a fast-moving vehicle.

Object lessons such as those remind us we must look at our surroundings to stay safe no matter how much we desire a treat along the way. We'll be run over if we waddle aimlessly through life unaware. Lingering too long on what our eyes desire can have deadly consequences.

A boulevard in central Florida

Another interesting sight was what appeared to be a blindfolded horse tied to a tree. Wow, was that image ever telling! At least the horse was in the shade. The tethered horse made us think about our freedom to choose how to live life rather than having our fate determined for us. Even with the gift of choice, are we choosing wisely or allowing our circumstances to dictate our destiny? If someone were riding by us, would they see us unencumbered to be and do all God wants for us, pursuing our calling with passion? Or would they see us living like a blindfolded horse tied to a tree, letting time slip by while waiting for the next meal or nap?

My final lesson that day appeared on a church marquee beside our hotel in Mount Dora, which read, "A closed mouth collects no foot." Reminders to watch what we say can keep us on track. Our words have the power to change lives—for better or worse. I find it challenging to choose my words wisely.

That day's lessons were striking reminders that making wise choices is both a privilege and a responsibility. When have you felt like that horse, or even the raven, stuck in a situation you didn't think you could escape, or languishing too long on risky or unhealthy things? Are you choosing your words carefully, to build up rather than tear down, to communicate love and caring rather than disparagement and negativity? The time is always right for a good decision.

As much as the wise counsel of our object lessons impressed us, the mere fact that we experienced them was even more profound. When you recognize those lessons as you journey through life, you know you're not alone and you're on the right track. God's presence speaks to us from all of His creation. There's no denying He is there.

For since the creation of the world His invisible attributes are clearly seen, being understood by the things that are made, even His eternal power and Godhead, so that they are without excuse.

ROMANS 1:20

Personal REFLECTION:

1. Think of a time when you chose your words poorly. If you had it to do all over again, what would you say?

2. Can you think of a time when God spoke to you through nature? What did He say?

3. Consider asking God to speak to you through nature in the upcoming days. If you're struggling with a particular problem, ask Him specifically about that. Then, make sure you are listening. It's a message you won't want to miss, even though you don't know precisely when and how it will come!

LESSON 42

"It's a God Thing"

You know you're in the right place when you experience
a divine encounter. Always look for them. They're more
prevalent than you might expect.

BY TIM

Debbie and I have had some of the most profound bicycle
touring experiences during our rest periods. On day eighty-
nine of TheHopeLine Tour, we had a rest day in Xenia,
Ohio, a hub for bicycling in that state. One of the several bicycle
paths that converge upon the town had brought us there. We would
ride out of town the next day on another. The trails were birthed
from old railroad beds in an area so flat that we couldn't help but
log many carefree miles before the next stop down the line.

Unfortunately, Xenia's flat terrain and proximity to midwestern
weather patterns make it a prime candidate for tornadoes. In fact,
the people of Xenia have some tragic tornado stories to tell. In one
of the most devastating tornadoes in US history, large sections of the
town were obliterated in 1974 as an F5 tornado erased them from the

map. Twenty-six years later, an F4 tornado touched down, meting out destruction and reminding residents of the risk in their environs. We're always intrigued by tornado stories, because, as bicycle tourists, we're particularly vulnerable to that type of adverse weather. It pays to know your enemy. Little did we realize as we ventured out for supper that we would soon hear about another form of destruction that is ravaging lives.

Ohio to Erie Trail

Our motel did not come with an accompanying restaurant, as many of them do. Our food choices were a half mile in one direction or one mile in the other direction. When the evening arrived, we were still scurrying around catching up on blogging. Even though we wanted to eat at a restaurant one mile down the road, we opted for the shorter and less time-consuming walk, the same one we had taken after we rolled into town the night before.

When we arrived at the eateries, we decided to check out a restaurant that specialized in chicken. Upon entering, however, we knew that it wouldn't be the place to carry on a meaningful conversation. Televisions hung from the ceiling in every direction, and *Monday Night Football* was blaring at an intolerable level. Although the menu intrigued us, we decided to depart for quieter surroundings.

Just outside the "chicken coop," we saw two more possibilities. One we had been to the night before. The other was a pizza joint. I asked Debbie which she preferred. She didn't really want pizza, so we decided to return to the restaurant with the broader menu.

Shortly after we'd sat down, a friendly waitress came to take our order. We told her we were bicycling across America. What had often followed in our conversation with strangers on TheHopeLine Tour happened again. We said we were both volunteer Hope Coaches for an organization called TheHopeLine, and that TheHopeLine had intervened in the lives of over three thousand young people who were struggling with suicidal thoughts in the prior year.

"Oh, this is a God thing!" she exclaimed.

Then, she sat down right next to Debbie and leaned into her. A crisis in her life was about to preempt our food order.

She told us her twenty-two-year-old son was talking about ending his life. He was struggling to see any purpose in living. She'd been encouraging him as best she could, but she was understandably concerned that her message was not taking root. We could tell she loved her son and was trying to parent well and appropriately, given his age. Sometimes, however, that's not enough. You can love, teach, model, and encourage, but you can't control the external influences in your adult children's lives, nor can you make their decisions for them. You also can't change the thoughts and feelings that run through them.

We tried to encourage her. First, we commended her for taking his claims seriously. She was showing him that she genuinely cared about him. Sadly, many young people who contact TheHopeLine don't receive this type of care and support from their parents. That's the first place where you would expect them to receive help, but often, parents are missing in action. We also encouraged her with a few success stories from TheHopeLine. When someone hears about miraculous interventions that hit close to home, it gives them hope that their own dire situation is not lost. Finally, we committed to praying for her son and gave her a card with TheHopeLine contact info to give to her son. Perhaps he would take it upon himself to reach out for help.

She was convinced God had sent us into that restaurant and even told her supervisor so. We didn't have much doubt ourselves, given how we'd arrived at this eatery yet again despite wanting another option. Simply being there was an encouragement to her—and to us. Evidently, she had been praying for God to intervene in her son's life, and she'd tuned her spiritual dial to look for an answer to those prayers. Somehow, our presence—on that day, at her table, in that restaurant, in that small Ohio town—played a role in her relationship with God and her personal crisis. Although we could see the circumstantial evidence of His timing, how God had orchestrated that divine encounter was beyond us. We'd traveled all the way from Oregon on bicycles and would be making our way farther east toward home in New England in search of encounters like this! How moving and humbling to sense that God was using us in response to someone else's prayers, especially those of a total stranger.

When you encourage others, you'll be encouraged. When God allows you the blessing of becoming His hands and feet, His eyes, ears, and mouth in a certain situation, you know He's real and He loves you. We had other experiences like that on TheHopeLine Tour. We were grateful God was directing our path and using us. It's comforting, yet humbling, to be part of a divine encounter. Not only did it keep the bicycle wheels spinning in a hopeful and meaningful direction on that tour, it also kept our own faith vibrant.

Are your eyes and ears open for encounters like that? I wonder how many of them come and go without us recognizing them. We get so preoccupied in our lives that we tend to miss what would otherwise be obvious. With the simplicity of a bicycle tour and the focus created by our mission to raise awareness and needed funds for TheHopeLine, the hubbub from our pre-tour lives was no longer drowning out God's "still, small voice." Sometimes, you need to make adjustments to hear it more clearly. Making a concerted effort to minister to the needs of others and cutting out some of the noise and the clutter can help. Then, watch the opportunities unfold and experience the blessedness of joining hands with your Creator. There's no better reason to live.

For it is God who works in you both to will and to do for His good pleasure.
PHILIPPIANS 2:13

Personal REFLECTION:

1. Think of someone who needs encouragement. How might you encourage that person this week?

2. Can you think of a time when you met a stranger's need because you were in the right place at the right time? Do you think it was a divine encounter?

3. Look for a divine encounter in the next week. Make yourself available and approachable. Slow down, look people in the eye, and express interest in them. Don't be surprised when they give you an opportunity to touch their lives.

LESSON 43

Coincidence

When coincidence becomes commonplace, you may
find yourself a bit befuddled, but God may be using you
for some divine purpose beyond your comprehension.

BY TIM

"Hey! Is this restaurant open?" inquired a portly, middle-aged man. He was sporting a wireless headset for the cell phone he had deposited into his shirt pocket. He had just broken the silence as he barged into the room. Several feet behind, his "better (and quieter) half" followed him.

"No, but you can get yourself a bowl of Cheerios," I retorted, pointing to the half-full dispenser on the other side of the room.

Debbie and I had begun our post-breakfast ritual in the otherwise empty room. We'd adopted that space as our living area when we weren't in our hotel room. It was formerly a restaurant situated off the hotel's lobby and served as the continental breakfast area for hotel guests. We'd been devoted patrons during our extended stay in Sioux City, Iowa, as we replenished our fuel stocks in hopeful anticipation of a return to the road.

The room had also doubled as our office for the past week, where we connected with people online and created content that helped tell the story of TheHopeLine Tour and the organization it was designed to help. We thought of that room as our "war room," where we were doing battle to motivate people and, ultimately, to effect change in the lives of young people in crisis. We'd called doctors, sent news releases, written blog posts, studied maps, and pitched emails from that room in efforts to make our fundraising thermometer rise. Anyone who ventured into our war room after breakfast hours had invaded our space!

"Have you ever seen one of these?" the man asked as he thrust his cell phone toward our table. Pictured on his iPhone was an unmistakable funnel cloud—the kind you see on The Weather Channel. "This was just last night on my property outside our home."

His wife moved toward our table too. I noticed she was carrying a folder with the name *Cargill* on it, which heightened my antennae. Inside were materials from a seminar the couple had attended. (Cargill is an agricultural conglomerate with a sizeable hedging business.) Apparently, they had landed in Sioux City for business reasons. They were a farming tandem.

"Do you hedge your price risk?" I asked.

It had happened again. Coincidence had become commonplace on that tour—all too coincidental and all too commonplace. I had just begun to proofread the chapter entitled "Weather" in a soon-to-be-released e-book I'd written, entitled *Hedging Commodity Price Risk: A Small Business Perspective.*

The couple sat down. We chatted about their storm-chasing activity the prior evening, midwestern weather, Cargill's pitch to increase their profits, and some of the logistics and risks pertaining to a corn and soybean farming operation. They had little to no experience with hedging but were investigating it further. These good folks were South Dakotans, so we found plenty to discuss, since we had crossed their home state by bicycle only days earlier. Not even their empty stomachs got in the way of our instant connection.

Eventually, they had to leave for their follow-up meeting at Cargill's office. Before they left, I shared a business card and a card for TheHopeLine Tour, along with a brief explanation of TheHopeLine itself.

"Contact me, and I'll send you a copy of my book," I told them.

Afterward, I asked Debbie, "What are the odds those two people would stumble into this room with two topics of such common interest: hedging commodity price risk and concerns about tornadoes?" Debbie nodded and smiled in complete agreement. We'd both been itching to get back on our bicycles. We were wondering why we weren't miles south in Missouri—or miles east in Massachusetts, for that matter. But, there we sat, in Sioux City, Iowa, with a stubborn injury to Debbie's calf and a stubborn resolve to get on with things, to finish what we had started and what we felt called to do for the benefit of young people in need.

Isn't it interesting when God designs impromptu meetings that leave you with no doubt He arranged them? When you encounter them on a regular basis, you begin to wonder if coincidence itself exists and whether the word is simply a convenient term for a skeptic. Merriam-Webster's says coincidence is accidental. Is it? After all, if you believe God is all-knowing and all-powerful and can control all of His creation, couldn't He choose to override the laws of nature He set in place and cause people whom He created to move in directions that bring about what we call coincidence? I find it even more interesting when I come away from those meetings asking, *God, what was that about?* I wonder if the other party knows the answer to that question and whether he or she also sensed that our chance encounter was not chance at all.

If you don't believe in God, how do you account for extraordinary coincidences, ones so prevalent and remarkable that it becomes difficult to believe they happened without some sort of supernatural intervention, whether they are occurring in your life or in someone else's?

As believers, Debbie and I had the comfort of knowing God was with us on the one hand, but on the other hand, we wondered what He was up to. Nevertheless, we were on a secure and adventurous journey, and we couldn't wait to find out what, or whom, we'd run into next.

Has coincidence become commonplace in your life? If so, Someone greater than you may be trying to get your attention—or keep it! Rather than running from it or trying to figure it out, take comfort in knowing that God loves you and will guide you. Resolve to walk with Him step by step as He directs you. Wait patiently for the next set of instructions. You're on the right track.

> **I will instruct you and teach you in the way you should go; I will guide you with My eye.**
>
> PSALM 32:8

Personal REFLECTION:

1. Is there such a thing as coincidence, or do you think God is orchestrating the timing of all human activity?

2. Think of a recent coincidence in your life. Did it bring about a blessing? Was there a greater purpose for why that coincidence happened?

3. The next time you have a coincidental encounter, resolve to ask the other party why they think you ran into each other.

LESSON 44

Encouragement Comes in Many Forms

Encouragement feeds a soul in pursuit of worthy goals.
You'll find it in most unexpected ways.

BY TIM

Our departure from a bed-and-breakfast in Whitehall, Montana, signaled the start to a brand-new day. We needed one. We'd developed some battle wounds from our first twenty-four days on TheHopeLine Tour. Our hands and rear ends were sore, and Debbie had burned her foot using the Jetboil on our last evening of camping. Our helmet camera had mysteriously disappeared, despite great efforts to find it. Furthermore, our newly acquired task of route planning had slowed us down.

So, a downhill ride at the start of a gorgeous day was ideal. Cycling through an area enclosed by large buttes with caverns added yet another feature to the unique Montana landscape. The scenery was absolutely fabulous. When a deer leapt over a fence and darted across the road in front of me, the joy of the ride kicked into high gear.

Magnificent!

We stopped for lunch in Three Forks, a western town with as wide a Main Street as they come—plenty of room for a gun duel or two out there, although we found the locals more than friendly. The town takes its name from the confluence of three rivers, which merge to form the Missouri River. We would be using that river as our guide for many miles of our trip down the road.

After lunch, we ventured out on a frontage road of I-90, eventually arriving in Belgrade on the outskirts of Bozeman around suppertime. Then, we had another divine encounter.

We met a family at Dairy Queen, and we conversed with them at length about TheHopeLine, our tour, and our lives. The patriarch, with his son-in-law, was doing prison ministry on a weekly basis. He expressed high interest in TheHopeLine and understood the value of it immediately. While Debbie chatted at length with his wife, I learned he was running a business that was at risk when commodity prices change. I shared some of what I know about the topic and gave him a draft copy of the e-book I'd been writing about hedging. We both seemed comfortable with and blessed by our rendezvous.

As the sun began to set, Debbie and I said good-bye to this warm family and headed to our motel for the evening. When we arrived, a welcome note entitled "To Our Guests" lay on our bed:

> In ancient times, there was a prayer for "The Stranger within our gates." Because this hotel is a human institution to serve people, and not solely a money making organization, we hope that God will grant you peace and rest while you are under our roof. May this suite and hotel be your "second" home. May those you love be near you in thoughts and dreams. Even though we may not know you, we hope that you will be comfortable and happy as if you were in your house. May the business that brought you our way prosper. May every call that you make and every message that you receive add to your joy. When you leave, may your journey be safe. We are all travelers. From "birth till death" we travel between eternities. May these days be pleasant for you, profitable for society, helpful for those you meet, and a joy to those who know and love you best.
>
> AUTHOR UNKNOWN

It's not often in this day and age that a business like that will invoke the name of God. Their warm and caring note reminded us that people were praying for our safety and our trip, and that we are never alone.

Encouragement comes in many forms. When it comes, pay homage to it. You can't get enough of it, and you can't proceed without it. We found it in no less than four ways that day. We ended the day feeling empowered. We were reminded that God's mercies are new every day. Debbie took two chats on TheHopeLine while I caught up on trip documentation. Although we bedded down late that evening, we were looking forward to yet another new day.

And lo, I am with you always, even to the end of the age.

MATTHEW 28:20B

Personal REFLECTION:

1. Why is encouragement such a valuable commodity?
2. Think of three different forms of encouragement that you received in the last week.
3. Think of a creative way to encourage someone in your life. Then, go do it.

LESSON 45

On Eagles' Wings

Some of God's creations model lessons for us simply
in how they move or behave. During trying times,
encouragement often descends right at the
appointed time!

BY DEBBIE

After starting our first tour as newlyweds and as novice bicycle tourists, the first few weeks were rough—to say the least. My body did not respond well to sitting on a bicycle seat eight hours a day. Tim and I were also discovering the challenge of being together 24/7 after being single for decades. Thankfully, the joy of following our passion of bicycling coupled with the surrounding beauty of the Pacific Northwest opened up our hearts and minds not to sweat the small stuff.

We left Missoula, Montana, early in the morning expecting a long day of pedaling. To be honest, I was intimidated, even a bit frightened, because I had a severe saddle sore that was hurting more each day. Two weeks of nonstop pedaling was taking its toll. We were somewhere in the Rocky Mountains, many miles, perhaps even days, from substantial services to the east. I was worried we might be nearing an end to this honeymoon on wheels.

Yet, just when we seemed to need it most, encouragement descended from above. First, it was a picture-perfect day in Montana. We were cycling under the bluest sky imaginable. Dazzling views of majestic mountains and the peaceful sounds of the Blackwater River were setting my mind at ease. I was amazed at the vast land and sky with unobstructed views of a grand and diverse terrain that one might expect to see in the centerfold of a nature magazine.

Then, shortly after lunch, I spotted some birds soaring high overhead, in stark contrast to their solid blue background. They were no ordinary birds. With large wings spread wide, they glided effortlessly, simply going with the flow. They seemed content to draw graceful, mountain-sized arcs above me. Soon, one appeared directly overhead. I stopped my bike, grabbed my camera, and stretched my arms skyward, clicking away and then showing my discovery to Tim, who had caught up to me. I could distinguish the bird's white head and brown body. It seemed eagles were watching over us! Tears and tingles overtook us as we absorbed the monumental moment. Later, we zoomed one of the pictures I had taken and marveled at the beauty of the bald eagle. Seeing an eagle was impressive enough. However, Tim and I have a special connection to what the eagle symbolizes, which made the sighting even more moving for us.

Before I was engaged to Tim, he told me about his special heart connection with a verse in the Bible that calls out this magnificent bird. I'd watched him live out that verse by waiting on the Lord for some major decisions in his life. God had also shown me that verse in very personal ways. We can read a passage of Scripture and live it out, but we don't often get the chance to experience it as an object lesson. I'd seen Google images of the eagle, read articles about it in *National Geographic* magazine, viewed photographs and drawings of our iconic national bird, and even seen one in captivity, but I'd never had a personal encounter with one in its natural setting—until then!

Our sighting demonstrated God's power and confirmed His love for us. We were feeling weak and vulnerable, and He was strengthening us with a visual sign of one of His truly remarkable creations. The eagle's elegant and stately flight demonstrated its giftedness. God was communicating with a combination of Scripture, imagery, and circumstances unique to us. We'd already been touched by references to the eagle individually, but now we'd experienced a supernatural encounter together as husband and wife!

Supernatural encounter

I'm so glad I took a photo of a sighting others can appreciate. The ease with which the eagle glided was a reminder to stay above the fray and to utilize and enjoy our God-given attributes. According to our special verse, the soaring image we'd just seen represents how we will behave as we look to God for strength and sustenance. He will elevate us out of difficulty, empower us with unusual strength and endurance, and bring us peace from life's frenetic pace.

Many people who believe in God like to encourage others by saying, "God is good all the time; all the time, God is good." It is easy to believe that on days like the day we saw eagles flying overhead in Montana. I believe God gives us days like that to remember when we are going through challenging times. We know He is with us based on what the Bible says, but sometimes we can lose sight of that. Recalling the "eagle-sighting days" will make the "cockroach-sighting days" much more bearable.

Every day, we are surrounded by God's beautiful creation, but most days, we miss it. We may be too busy running around, staring at our navel, or looking through blinders. Watching a sunrise or sunset, checking out the phases of the moon, or looking for the spectacular from nature is not a daily priority for most people. If we happen to notice the unusual or astounding around us, great, but if not, we don't seem to think much about it. On many of our bike rides, we have seen God's beauty up close and personal. A handful of those times, however, have truly been showstoppers.

Are you stopping to look "skyward" for the encouragement that comes from above? It will be there whether or not you're ready to receive it. You'll enjoy the benefit of God's presence most when you're watchful. The next time you need a strong dose of encouragement, take the time to look for it. God speaks to you in your own unique language. He knows how to touch you, if only you will give Him your attention. Let His touch sustain you as you continue on your journey through life.

. . . .

But those who wait on the LORD shall renew their strength; they shall mount up with wings like eagles, they shall run and not be weary, they shall walk and not faint.

ISAIAH 40:31

. . . .

Personal REFLECTION:

1. What particular aspects of creation move you?

2. What reaction do you have when you experience what moves you? What emotions do you feel? What thoughts go through your mind?

3. Sometime in the next week, seek out a part of creation that moves you so you can experience it anew. When you experience it, record the blessing in some fashion.

LESSON 46

New Beginnings

Significant pursuits come in phases, because we can only endure so much effort and intensity at a time. When you begin a new phase, you've just claimed your second wind. You'll find strength and power that might have been lacking.

BY TIM

There was a psychological effect to crossing the Mississippi River on TheHopeLine Tour. Simply by cycling across the bridge, we had moved to "our" side of the country and were heading home. The Wild West was long gone, and we were returning to more familiar ground. Crossing the Mississippi changed our perspective.

That day brimmed with new beginnings. Early in the day, we'd cycled into downtown Cape Girardeau, Missouri, where we first glimpsed the river that divides America for east-west travelers. We were reminded of the new beginning immediately upon entering Illinois. A large, flat floodplain with bountiful crops preparing for harvest had replaced the rolling hills of Missouri. Even after several miles in our new state, we could look back and see the bridge that spans the Mississippi, which acted as a splendid backdrop for the expansive fields.

Headed home

Just outside of Ullin, Illinois, a young man came into the restaurant where Debbie and I were finishing up our lunch. He had sought us out after seeing our bicycles outside labeled with "TheHopeLine" signs. Debbie went to the restroom while I spoke with him.

"Do you have time to talk?" he asked.

"Sure!" I said.

He asked me about our tour and about TheHopeLine. TheHopeLine intrigued him, because he had converted to Christianity after a life of drug abuse and other bad decisions. His spiritual awakening had delivered him from those issues. Because of his past, in no time and with little explanation, he understood what TheHopeLine does and why it works.

He was passionate about adventure as well as his Christian faith. His exuberance fueled mine. It reminded me of our purpose on that bicycle tour. Many people with whom we had shared our mission listened politely. They might have made supportive comments, or they might only have listened and kept their thoughts to themselves. Some simply needed time to process and investigate what we'd presented to them.

However, few people exuded the type of passion that this man showed. His attitude renewed my outlook on why we were sharing information about TheHopeLine.

God was reminding me yet again that He was placing certain people in our path. That encouraged me to keep "sowing the seed" and convinced me that our volunteer efforts were not in vain. That new beginning was right on time. When we returned to the road after lunch, it seemed we were cycling faster with less effort! We had just been jump-started.

Some youth who contact TheHopeLine are due for a new beginning. It's why they reach out in the first place. Some are eager to embrace it, while others haven't yet mustered the courage to take the plunge. Those who are desperate enough will grab hold of the new beginning, which usually means deciding to change course. They may realize a destructive habit needs to go. Perhaps they need a relationship change. Some may even realize they need a new spiritual beginning. Whatever the case, when new beginnings come to those who reach out, they'll be traveling toward a predetermined destination, similar to what we do on any bicycle tour.

New beginnings in life bring clarity. We all need them from time to time to remind us where we should be going, to renew our perspective, and to refresh our approach. They may come in the form of a new hobby, a new job, a new home, a new marital status, a new locale, perhaps even a new idea or simply a resolve to make a needed change. Fresh starts can often accelerate personal growth or jump-start us when we are stuck. Welcome them when they come. Better yet, pursue them with all the vigor you can muster.

Behold, God is my helper; the Lord is with those who uphold my life.

PSALM 54:4

Personal REFLECTION:

1. In what facet of your life do you need a new beginning?

2. What activity can you pursue or what book can you read to remind you of or reinforce the purpose in your journey?

3. With whom can you talk to help you look at your circumstances from a fresh perspective?

LESSON 47

Recognizing a Blessing

Unusual events with impeccable timing affirm that your
Tour Guide is at work on your behalf.

BY TIM

Each of our tours seemed to take on its own character. Early on, the
Mom-to-Mom Tour up the Atlantic coast was all about beating
the heat by burning up mileage on flat terrain. We'd even eclipsed
one hundred miles in one day in Georgia. By the time we made it to
North Carolina, we'd grown a bit impatient with zigzagging on secondary
roads. It had begun to feel like we were making little progress despite the
many miles we had cycled. Although we enjoy casual touring, we needed
to make more headway.

Day nineteen preceded a Sunday, which we were targeting for a
rest day. So we opted for another early start to maximize some quality
riding on the main drag, which was a more direct route than the one
our bicycling maps showed us. Besides, the usual weekday traffic would
be sleeping in on a Saturday.

Off we went, shortly after seven o'clock in the morning, cycling north on US Route 17 out of Wilmington, North Carolina. Beachgoers and golfers were out early, yet traffic was thin, and the four-lane divided highway allowed us plenty of space. A gentle tailwind was an added bonus.

We had chewed up over fifty miles before our noontime lunch stop outside of Jacksonville. Swift passage through Saturday's nearly vacant streets brought us to a shopping-area sub shop.

After an enjoyable and reinvigorating break, we knew we had more good miles within us, especially with our upcoming rest day awaiting us. We decided to defer booking an overnight stay until we approached services. We liked to stay close to ample restaurants before a rest day and a church before a Sunday. New Bern seemed like a reasonable goal. Certainly, a chain motel would pop up on a commercial strip there, where we could add points to a rewards program.

With more zigzagging ahead on the bicycle maps, we decided to go the direct route again and then finish the day on less-traveled roads. The final stretch would provide some relief for the frayed nerves and spent muscles that were sure to arise from our lengthy stretch of highway riding.

Nine miles short of New Bern, we heard the first of many rumbles in the distance. We had noticed—and been thankful for—some cloud activity overhead and to the north since midday. The cloud cover had alleviated the oppressive heat wave. Yet we had become familiar enough with these summertime weather patterns to know that we should be close to cover when dark clouds and heat collide.

As we approached town with over ninety miles on the day, the impending storm was nearing its boiling point. The sky had grown extremely dark even though the sun had not yet set. The rumbles of thunder were louder and more frequent. We parked roadside to check the GPS for motel accommodations and placed several phone calls to chain motels. The prices they quoted triggered sticker shock. Some of those motels were only a mile away, while most were three miles away in another direction. One phone call even resulted in no answer. How could motels do business if they didn't even pick up the phone?

We decided to travel to the motels that were over three miles away, because they seemed more plentiful and we assumed they would offer plenty of nearby services. So, we continued under ever more ominous storm clouds.

Within a half mile, we came to a major interchange with lengthy bridges over what we later learned was the Neuse River basin. I didn't want to backtrack over any of those bridges, particularly in a storm. Our GPS pointed us toward one of two large bridges, but we noticed a motel a short distance to our left. The name looked familiar, because it had come up on our GPS as the nearest listing.

"Let's give this one a shot," I said.

With a clean, modern appearance, a restaurant nearby, and with dark clouds looming overhead, the motel appealed to us. We called the front desk and were pleasantly surprised by their low price, complete with breakfast. With the sky growing blacker by the second, we rode to the motel and checked in. Moments later, the skies let loose. A long, electrical storm ensued. We had escaped it!

Sometimes, God offers us choices that are right in front of us, yet we have difficulty recognizing them, even when dark clouds loom. By His grace, He takes our best efforts by the hand and leads us. When the circumstances are unusual and timed perfectly, little doubt remains that He has intervened. Debbie and I experienced one such moment on that day. That motel was within walking distance of the historic downtown region, which hosted several churches. Later, we learned the other motels had no churches within walking distance. Our room was perfect, better than many of the ones we'd stayed in at more expensive chain motels.

Remain open to the possibilities God places right before you. Heed them well, for they may be heaven-sent blessings in subtle packaging. Sometimes, distractions and the pace of life can make these blessings hard to recognize, but keep an eye out for them anyway. You won't want to let them slip through your hands.

....

A man's heart plans his way, but the LORD directs his steps.

PROVERBS 16:9

....

Personal REFLECTION:

1. When was the last time you missed an "obvious" opportunity? Why do you think you missed it?

2. How might you build flexibility in your planning to allow for last-minute changes?

3. Consider adopting a looser schedule to allow for the best that life has to offer.

LESSON 48

God's Perfect Timing

When circumstances conspire to bring about unusual
blessings, be quick to assign credit to the only possible
Source. These miracles often arise when you least
expect them. Keep them close to your heart. They'll
act as constant reminders that you are not alone.

BY DEBBIE

While we were cycling east out of the Badlands in South
Dakota on TheHopeLine Tour, Tim and I talked about
how meaningful it would be to attend TheHopeLine's
"Prayer for a Generation" event coming up in Sioux Falls, South
Dakota, in ten days. We could join with personnel from the
TheHopeLine and other concerned people in the region who wanted
to make a difference for this generation. We were cycling in that
direction, but once we hit the Missouri River, our route would take
us southeast instead. And our timing just wasn't right. We'd need
to wait around for a week, which would delay our entire trek across
America. So, we cycled due east to Chamberlain and then hopped
on ACA's Lewis & Clark Trail toward the Nebraska border and away
from Sioux Falls.

I began to notice some swelling and pain in my right calf. At first, it wasn't too bad, so I kept going. When we arrived in Yankton, though, the swelling and pain had become more noticeable. Some conversations with people there and in Vermillion the next day suggested that a short, flat ride to Sioux City, Iowa, would land us at the best medical services in the area to have it checked out. Meanwhile, I'd gone online and diagnosed the problem on my own: a stress fracture or shin splints.

After arriving in Sioux City on Sunday afternoon, we scheduled a Tuesday appointment with an orthopedic doctor to confirm my diagnosis. The appointment was at eight thirty in the morning, because I was hoping we could get back to the hotel, check out, and be on our way afterward.

No such luck!

The doctor's diagnosis of my condition was neither a stress fracture nor shin splits. It was chronic compartment syndrome, which is common in athletes under the age of thirty, mostly runners, not bicyclists. I wasn't under thirty, and I hadn't run in years, so the diagnosis made no sense. The doctor recommended a reevaluation after at least a week of rest and lots of ibuprofen. Rest for a week? I had never done such a thing!

Regardless, God works in mysterious ways, and His timing is always perfect. We had bicycled 2,296 miles thus far on TheHopeLine Tour. My injury could have happened anywhere along our journey, especially after climbing the Bighorn Mountains in Wyoming, McKenzie Pass in Oregon, or the rolling hills of South Dakota ten days earlier. But it happened there in the flatlands, just as we were about to cycle far away from South Dakota.

When we shared my diagnosis with one contact at TheHopeLine, he said, "How can we get you to Sioux Falls?" Prayer for a Generation was only eighty miles away that Friday evening. They wanted us at the event, where they would share our mission with others at a pre-event dinner.

Prayer for a Generation would focus on praying for teens and young adults growing up in the world today. Attendees would be praying for them to seek God and find the love, hope, and faith that come from a relationship with Jesus. For those who had already made their peace with God, attendees would ask God to raise up from among them strong leaders who could come alongside peers in need.

So, Friday's "date night" was looking better than ever. We rented a car and headed north to Sioux Falls. We hadn't traveled in an automobile for seven weeks, so the first several miles were an adjustment as we sped by a portion of the route we had taken on our bicycles five days earlier. By the time we arrived in Sioux Falls, what would have taken us all day on our bikes took only seventy minutes by car!

As we walked into Central Baptist Church, the site of the dinner and Prayer for a Generation event, excitement and anticipation bubbled up within me. Sporting our matching TheHopeLine shirts, Tim and I met some people who recognized us instantly from our tour's media coverage out of Sioux City.

Soon, we met Dawson McAllister, founder of TheHopeLine; Tim Altman, CEO of the organization that runs the TheHopeLine; and other personnel connected with the organization. Sioux Falls hosts a call center for TheHopeLine, so we also met some people who worked there and with whom we engaged regularly as remote volunteer Hope Coaches.

At the dinner, longtime supporters were recognized for their commitment to TheHopeLine. We heard stories from Dawson McAllister's forty-plus years of helping youth in crisis. Seated at our table was a man who had known Dawson since he started in youth ministry years ago. We met other Hope Coaches and listened to their gratitude for being able to serve in this ministry. The dinner was delightful, but underneath it was a tone of deep concern for this nation's youth. One statement startled me: we are only one generation away from losing the church.

After dinner, we joined about four hundred people of all ages already gathered in the large auditorium for worship, the program, and prayer. It was powerful. The praise band led us in worship. Tim Altman presided thereafter, and Dawson McAllister, who has devoted his entire life to helping young people, addressed the crowd.

I loved the interaction between Dawson and the audience. He asked people to share stories about those who had prayed for them over the years. The point? People who overcome problems have had someone praying for them. Several young people cited aunts and uncles. A grandmother, a parent, and a spouse were important prayer warriors for others. Many youth had abandoned their faith for a time, some had been addicted, and two girls said they'd been raped. Yet all were on the road to recovery. Their transparency amazed me, but their gratitude did not surprise me. What a privilege it was to hear the evidence of answered prayers: marriages mended, addictions annihilated, hearts healed, lives restored. Only God could do all of that.

After Dawson spoke, several leaders in the Sioux Falls faith community led us in prayer. A Hope Coach prayed for the young people who already knew and followed God. A University of Sioux Falls educator and a campus minister prayed for the teachers, principals, and administrators who would be starting school in the coming week. Another leader prayed for hurting and hopeless young people in dire need of help. Yet another prayed for youth pastors and ministers. Finally, a humble prayer warrior prayed that God's extravagant love would ignite a mass movement of faith in Jesus across the nation. We ended the evening by gathering in small groups and praying for today's generation of young people.

Upon departing, we discovered exhibits in the lobby for many youth ministries that serviced the Sioux Falls region. Imagine if we started praying for, helping, and loving the youth in America on a daily basis. Imagine helping to save the lives of troubled youth so they could know God, follow Him, and make a difference with their peers!

The effect of one night of prayer pales in comparison to what daily prayers will do for this generation. Most experts agree that all revivals and spiritual awakenings begin with prayer. God makes a promise in 2 Chronicles 7:14—"If My people who are called by My name will humble themselves, and pray and seek My face, and turn from their wicked ways, then I will hear from heaven, and will forgive their sin and heal their land." Will you join us in praying for this generation?

Tim and I were grateful my health issue developed in Sioux City, so close to that event. As I said, God's perfect timing always comes through. We were also thankful for that time of rest. I could have easily felt sorry for myself with my leg condition. However, since we'd arrived in Sioux City, we were on local television, in the *Sioux City Journal*, and on a radio interview in Maine. Those media connections allowed us to share about TheHopeLine Tour and our desire to raise $100,000 to help young people from ages thirteen to twenty-nine. The outpouring of God's provision also showed forth one morning that week when, to our amazement, $1,700 in donations to TheHopeLine rolled into our inboxes from people connected to Tim's former employer.

Sometimes, when our plans appear thwarted, God has something better in mind. Our hearts' desire is to see a revival in this generation of young people. Little did we know we'd be spending some time at that event with some prominent leaders and several hundred other people who shared the same desire and vision. When you delight yourself in the Lord, He will grant you the desires of your heart. The timing of our trek across South Dakota had set the stage for a glimpse of what it would take to see our hearts' desire come to fruition.

As for God, His way is perfect; the word of the Lord is proven; He is a shield to all who trust in Him.

PSALM 18:30

Personal REFLECTION:

1. Can you think of a relative, a friend, or a mentor who prayed for you when you were younger? What effect do you think their prayers have had on your life?

2. Is there a young person in your life who could benefit from your consistent and thoughtful prayers? Set aside time each day to pray for that person.

3. Think about a strong, unfulfilled desire you have. Have you ever considered that it hasn't happened yet because the timing isn't right? Be thankful that it may still come to pass in due time. Pray toward that end. "Delight yourself also in the Lord, and He shall give you the desires of your heart" (Psalm 37:4).

LESSON 49

Unexpected Blessing

Welcome unexpected affirmations whenever you can.
They will fortify and sustain you on your path ahead.

BY TIM

On day thirty-nine of our honeymoon tour, we had escaped some lightning and storms on a sultry midwestern August afternoon. The following morning, a thunderstorm ripped through Streator, Illinois, where we were staying, and cleared the air. Once on the road, we discovered the storm had also rectified the wind. Finally, it was blowing in our favor. We would be cycling in a flatlander's paradise with only one hundred miles of cornfields separating us from Rensselaer, Indiana. The time was ripe for our first touring century (a bicycle ride of at least one hundred miles in one day).

Debbie called her principal that morning. We were still new at projecting our progress, but our best guess suggested she might be late for her return to the classroom. He extended her some grace, but a timely return to her teaching obligation was an added incentive to churn out ever-increasing daily mileage on the flat terrain.

We headed east out of Streator and worked our way onto Route 17. We were screaming ahead with the tailwind and the smooth, flat road, with no vehicles in sight. After some thirty miles of cruising, we crossed I-55 and Old Route 66 and entered the town of Dwight. A road sign near a correctional institution on the outskirts of town suggested travelers not pick up hitchhikers. We weren't stopping for anything except a bathroom break or a snack. Not even a prison escapee was going to slow us down.

Flatlander's paradise in the Midwest

Though it was still early in the day, the temperature had already eclipsed 90 degrees. We cycled straight through Dwight and turned right onto an isolated road amid more cornfields. The road had some tar patch covering up cracks in the pavement. My tire tread left its imprint in the soft tar, which was liquefying in the extreme heat. The sticky tar left its mark as well. Pebbles clung to our tires, begging for a clean sweep every few miles. However, such frequent housekeeping was not in the cards that day.

As we continued to crank out the heat-infested miles, I began to hear a flapping sound, which emanated from the road upon every revolution of my front wheel. I wasn't inclined to stop to examine the wheel until I had to. However, as we burned off more miles, the sound became louder.

We arrived at the tiny farming community of Cabery, which gave us opportunity for a cold drink and a breather. The townsfolk were huddled at the general store we had entered in search of the cooler. It seemed not much had changed in Cabery over the years, certainly not the interior of the store. Conversations about crops and weather filled the air much as they might have twenty, forty, or one hundred years earlier. We were simply intent on doing our business and heading for the next grain elevator to the east. We were on pace for a record-setting day.

"There's a detour down the road, but you can ride around it," one local said. "Just go one side or the other when you come to the bridge repair sign. It will only cost you an extra mile or two. You'll be heading around a big field."

We thanked him and then carried on. Soon, sure enough, there was the sign: "Detour Ahead, Bridge Repair." We turned right and cycled along yet another massive field with corn so robust we thought we might hear it growing. We took the next two left turns and found the original route on the other side of the bridge outage. We turned right and were back on track.

Meanwhile, I could ignore the noise from my wheel no longer. The tire was failing. After two thousand miles in some intense riding conditions like that day, the tread was pulling away from its core. I didn't want to ride late in the day with that issue despite the possibility of forfeiting our intended century.

Around four thirty, we arrived in Chebanse for supper. I needed to call a bicycle shop before they closed for the day. Our maps provided contact information for bicycle repair services, but there were few of them. I dialed a couple of the numbers across the border in Indiana, but no one answered. However, a shop to the north, in Bradley, Illinois, picked up my call.

Steve, the owner of Tern of the Wheel, had not only one but four new tires, the same brand and model as we had on our bicycles. Furthermore, he offered to bring them to his home in Kankakee, which was closer to us than his shop, and to install them for us! How could we refuse such an offer? When we arrived at Steve's house, he and his wife, Joan, invited us to stay for supper and for the night.

Despite our desire for a long day in the saddle, our diversion to Kankakee and the hospitality of our hosts brought an unexpected blessing. That day's goal of cycling one hundred miles would become the next day's dream. Steve and Joan's kindness provided for us far beyond what we expected or deserved. We wouldn't need to worry about tire failure for the remainder of our trip. And we enjoyed good conversation and free room and board for the evening!

The best blessings in life are often the unplanned ones. Heaven-sent provisions we could never arrange remind us that we have limited control over our own destiny in spite of our free will.

When external forces beyond your control thrust you forward in your journey, you'll be left with no doubt that you're on the right track. Someone is looking out for you.

> **For the Lord is good; His mercy is everlasting, and His truth endures to all generations.**
> PSALM 100:5

Personal REFLECTION:

1. Think of a time when an unexpected blessing came your way at the cost of altering your plans. Was it worth it?

2. Think of a time when alternatives to your plans came your way but you stuck with your plans anyway and paid a price. What would you do differently the next time?

3. How do you think unexpected blessings occur? Are they the result of Someone looking out for you, or do they happen randomly and by chance?

LESSON 50

Rising to New Heights

Ambitious challenges produce monumental results.
Welcome them enthusiastically. When you've conquered
them, take note. You can do more than you
thought or imagined. And you are capable of
even bigger and better!

BY TIM

Debbie and I had our work cut out for us. We were ninety miles away from the next set of services. The Bighorn National Forest—and a 9,600-foot mountain pass—stood in our way. We'd never cycled above seven thousand feet of elevation. What's more, we'd just bicycled 156 miles in 90-degree heat the previous two days on TheHopeLine Tour.

An early start that day was imperative. For some reason, my cell phone, which doubled as our alarm clock, was an hour fast. That seemed unusual, since cell phone clocks update automatically with time-zone changes. Regardless, when the alarm went off at five thirty, we arose an hour earlier than planned. It turned out to be a good thing!

After a large breakfast at McDonald's, we left Worland, Wyoming, in search of higher ground. Our final intended destination on that day was Buffalo, Wyoming, but only after we would ascend Powder River Pass. A local had told us we could divide our ride into thirds. The first third would be flat, the second third would be a steady climb, and the final third would be entirely downhill. He was right about the climb but wrong on the other two counts.

Bighorn National Forest ahead in Wyoming

The "flat" portion of our day was really a set of rolling hills. Sure, we had little change in altitude after completing it, but we climbed several hills during that stretch. The terrain was fascinating, just what you might expect to see on the moon or another planet, the type of terrain we'd come to appreciate in Wyoming. A herd of pronghorn showed up early in the morning as a tease for what was to come.

The day's middle leg, the gradual climb, was true to form, and we cycled it for seven hours. Climbing with a heavy load is slow. We were thrilled, however, to eclipse the mountain pass at six o'clock.

The final leg of our journey also came with some surprises. Due to more rolling hills, we climbed another one thousand feet before our free fall into Buffalo. After a day of trudging up an estimated nine thousand feet of elevation, we felt like large boulders that had been nudged to the edge of the cliff and, with one last tap, sent over the edge. Maximum speeds with our oversized loads approached forty miles per hour. The data is estimated, because our ten-hour cycling day, with over thirteen hours on the road from start to finish, outlasted our GPS's battery life.

We assumed the final thirty-five miles of our day would be easy, all downhill, but what did we know? In a cruel twist of fate, the one thousand feet of additional climbing was thrust between our premature mountaintop celebration and the plunging joyride ahead. To top it off, our fluids were running low, as was daylight.

After cycling through the Rockies and coming to high plains in central Montana and Wyoming, how did this mountain range pop up to become such a lofty impediment to east-west travel through the state of Wyoming? Its physical features do not mesh with the surrounding plains. The Bighorn is a place unto itself.

Earlier in the day, as we approached Bighorn Range, we had cycled through barren buttes filled with untapped minerals. There were no trees and not many shrubs, at least until we began our climb. Where we come from, God placed the forest at the base of the mountains. If you go high enough, you break the tree line where trees give way to rocks. The Bighorn National Forest works in reverse. As we climbed, we began to see vegetation. Eventually, trees popped up. When we had reached seven thousand feet, we were in the midst of a full-fledged forest.

The grade and length of the climb were also noteworthy. Another local had told us to expect a 6 percent grade for thirty miles, which felt quite accurate by six o'clock. The grade had twisted through the Ten Sleep River Canyon at its base and, eventually, the climb straightened out. The diversity of the terrain added joy and awe to our experience.

On the final thirty-mile leg, vistas of grand, snowcapped mountains wowed us. The beautiful views appeared intermittently as we twisted up and down the punishing hills. On our ten-mile descent into Buffalo, green, velvet-like, rolling hills had supplanted the barren landscape of daybreak. Shadows from the setting sun accentuated their plush appearance.

The Bighorn region was an unexpected treat. Despite never having climbed above seven thousand feet of altitude before, on that day we were rising to new heights. We topped 9,600 feet on a day in which we cycled over ninety miles. We never knew we could do such a thing. Sore hands and butts notwithstanding, it was a mountaintop experience in every sense of the word.

When you undertake a grand adventure, you're never certain what to expect. Such is the nature of adventure. Had we known what lay before us, we may have had stronger doubts about our ability to accomplish that feat. However, we learned we could do more than we realized, which suggests we have even more capabilities within us. Never let a lack of confidence limit what you yearn to achieve. Chances are you're under-estimating your capacity and will miss out if you don't follow through. When you do tackle something big and the results surprise you, let it be a lesson that you can rise to higher heights in the future if you are willing to attempt the climb.

I can do all things through Christ who strengthens me.

PHILIPPIANS 4:13

Personal REFLECTION:

1. Have you ever felt intimidated by a challenge you were facing? What was your response?

2. When was the last time you attempted something that seemed unattainable?

3. Do you have a dream you've set aside because you lack confidence? Is it time to dust off the dream and consider how you might begin to pursue it?

LESSON 51

An Abrupt End

Regardless of whether or not you reach your intended
destination, the end of any worthy journey will bring its
own special stamp of affirmation.

BY TIM

I t wasn't supposed to end like it did. A beautiful day, a visit to a
church, and a short ride of twenty-five miles to a waiting motel room
were supposed to bring us to a couple of rest days. We planned to
catch up on some loose ends, make some more pitches in support of
TheHopeLine, and catapult into the final week or so of our tour and our
arrival at the Atlantic Ocean. However, we don't get to write the script
to our adventures—or to life, for that matter.

A few miles out of Troy, Pennsylvania, Debbie took a spill on her
bicycle. When I looked up from a few hundred feet behind and saw her
tumble, I wasn't sure what had happened. Knowing Debbie, I expected
her to pull herself up and continue. She did the first part, but when she
tried the second, she winced in pain. She thought she might have broken
a bone. Naturally, the uncertainty of what that might mean for the rest
of our trip tugged at her emotions—and at mine.

Falls like this are common in bicycling. It could have happened anywhere, at any time, and it could have happened to me. Why it happened to Debbie at that moment, merely a few hundred miles from the finish line, only God knows.

We pulled ourselves aside to regroup. When Debbie flexed her arm slowly and winced at the extreme pain, we were both concerned about her ability to ride for help. Soon, a vehicle slowed down, and the woman in the passenger seat asked if we needed help.

"Yes!" Debbie said without hesitation.

What was about to unfold would be among the most moving acts of kindness and understanding we'd ever received in our many miles of bicycle touring. Our Good Samaritans were about to dramatically change the complexion of what would be the final day of bicycling on TheHopeLine Tour.

As we stood by, stunned at what had happened, our Good Samaritan "SWAT team" of three mobilized, bringing our would-be crash landing to an ever-so-gentle transition back to ordinary life. They operated with the speed and efficiency of skilled bike mechanics, the tenacity of Kentucky dogs in pursuit of bicycles, and the grace of dedicated Christ-followers. At day's end, Debbie and I had to enumerate the incredible events in order to take it all in. (Debbie will elaborate on the care and kindness of those angels in our next and final lesson from the road.)

Over the past week or so, we'd found ourselves cycling in the land of paradox, where we wanted to bring that long tour to a triumphant and fulfilling finish, yet didn't want the experience to end. Even after 4,300 miles, how could we wish away brand-new days in new places with new faces, feeling the ever-present touch of God's hand on our journey? Yet the physical and mental demands to be "on our game" every waking hour—and too many waking hours to contend with—had taken their toll. It was an intense tour, which augmented both the challenge and the reward. We loved it.

We couldn't have picked a finer day to conclude our tour, nor finer people to end it with. When we walked out of the hospital emergency room with our fate sealed in the cast upon Debbie's right arm, the beauty of the sun casting its spotlight on thousands of multicolored trees on the Pennsylvania hills reminded us that all was still well. And with an overflow of love and care from our guardian angels, who had arrived on the scene too soon for the intended finale yet right on time, we felt the gentleness of God's provision setting us at rest. It was a day we will never forget!

What lies around the next corner in your life?

In spite of the circumstances, Debbie was feeling okay. And despite the obvious disappointment at the abrupt end of our tour and not reaching our intended destination, we were overwhelmed with gratitude for the phenomenal experiences we'd been privileged to share on TheHopeLine Tour. It was a powerful time of blessing, and its ending validated its beginning. We'd envisioned a triumphant ending, and even though it was not as we expected, God certainly delivered on it. It was a fitting climax too. After all, the glory was His, not ours.

Sometimes, you will not make it to your destination. That's why it's important to embrace the challenge and enjoy the journey along the way. Whether or not you achieve your goal need not diminish your satisfaction. When you set big goals and strive to achieve them, don't let them define success for you. Although you have your own idea of what should come about, God may have a different one. And you may never know why. If you base your self-worth and your definition of success on achieving your goals, you may end up bitterly disappointed.

Instead, ask yourself if you gave it your all. If you did, then you accomplished much in your adventure, even though not what you had envisioned. I dare say you're a better individual for having pursued your dreams with passion. Look at what you were allowed to experience, what you learned, and whom you enjoyed life with along the way. God is more interested in developing your character than your ego. When your plans honor Him, when you pursue them with all you have, and when you commit the results to Him, you cannot fail.

"For My thoughts are not your thoughts,
nor are your ways My ways," says the Lord.

ISAIAH 55:8

Personal REFLECTION:

1. Are you disappointed about something you were unable to achieve? Can you think of any redeeming qualities of the experience?

2. When you consider your greatest achievements and your near misses, which of your character attributes grew as a result of each? Did you learn new skills? How have you used those attributes and skills in subsequent endeavors?

3. Have windows of opportunity opened for you after failed attempts to achieve a goal, allowing you to move on with a sense of completion? If not, how might you approach the goal differently to achieve it?

LESSON 52

Beauty from Ashes

You cannot travel through life alone. Sooner or later, you
will need the help of those around you. And when total
strangers come to your aid, you'll recognize the hand of
God on your pursuit.

BY DEBBIE

At breakfast at McDonald's after church, it hit me: the end was
in sight! Tim had just explained that we probably had only
seven or eight riding days left before arriving at the Atlantic
Ocean. As much as I wanted to be home, and as tired as I was after 102
days on the road, I felt sad TheHopeLine Tour would soon be ending. I
was so looking forward to the two days of rest just ahead to prepare us
for the homestretch. With 4,336 miles behind us, we were 90 percent of
the way home. The shortest ride of our tour thus far, twenty to twenty-
five miles, would get us to our rest days.

After breakfast, we headed toward Towanda, Pennsylvania, on
US Route 6. The beauty of northern Pennsylvania in the peak of
foliage season was breathtaking. The day seemed warmer than the
past week, when we wore three to five layers of clothing to ward off
the morning chill.

As I ascended a slight grade along a narrow portion of road, I grazed the guardrail with my right rear pannier. Then, I swerved left and straightened my bike, only to hit a loose rock on the shoulder with my front tire. Down I went, right into the travel lane. Thankfully, no cars were speeding up behind me, which gave me time to pick myself up and get out of the road. When I moved my right arm though, I heard a crackling sound, which triggered a well of emotions. As bad as my arm hurt, another feeling haunted me: *Is the remainder of our bicycling adventure in jeopardy?*

Meanwhile, cars and trucks continued to speed by on the other side of the road. Eventually, one of those cars turned around, and its occupants came back to check on us. The vehicle slowed down as it approached, and the woman on the passenger side asked if I needed help. They continued down the road to turn around while Tim moved our bicycles to a wider portion of the road. The carful of would-be rescuers met us there.

When the woman, Amy, and her husband, Gary, got out of their car, I felt a calm come over me. Their countenances radiated joy and contentment. Gary said they had just come from church and were on their way home to Canton. They saw me fall and came back to see if we needed help. Somehow, I felt an instant connection between the four of us.

"Whatever you need, we'll see that you get it," Amy said. She looked me straight in the eye with a compassion you don't see every day. The peace grew within me.

As our conversation unfolded, they seemed to know exactly what we needed, yet they respected our decision-making while offering information about local services. The more time we spent with them, it became apparent to us that they also understood what we were feeling. Soon, I found out they were both in education, so we would have plenty to talk about as we spent the rest of the day together.

Their four-passenger Subaru would not fit our bicycles and gear, so Gary called their neighbor, Jeff, who was watching his son's soccer game. Jeff arrived in no time with a clean and capable pickup truck to transport us to the hospital. He hopped out of his truck and joined Gary and his son. They picked up our bicycles, loaded panniers and all, as if they were children's tricycles and placed them in the back of the pickup.

When we arrived at the emergency room at the hospital in Troy, the security guard asked me to fill out a simple form before admitting me. With Tim by my side, a kind nurse attended to me within two minutes of arriving. With only one other patient seeking medical attention, I saw the doctor almost immediately. Emergency room service that fast and friendly doesn't happen every day. It added yet another blessing to a day filled with them. The radiologist who read the X-ray concurred with the doctor. I had chipped my radius. They put my arm in a cast, and the doctor recommended I see an orthopedic surgeon within a few days.

Unbeknownst to me, our Good Samaritans had been waiting outside for a couple of hours on a "football Sunday." They had called their pastor, who had joined them, and they had already placed us on their church's prayer chain!

I came outside and saw them basking in the late-afternoon sun. As I looked at the blue sky and the colorful trees displaying their autumn regalia on the nearby hills, I thought, *This must be what heaven is like: surrounded by loving people in a beautiful setting.*

I looked back and saw the other patient leave the emergency room with a sling on his arm.

"What is this? One-size-fits-all treatment?" I joked.

He said he had popped a tendon in his right arm while bowling. His parents asked what had happened to me. I told them we were bicycling across the country raising money for TheHopeLine. I described our goal to raise $100,000 for this organization with its focus of preventing suicide among young people. The woman's eyes filled with tears as she spoke of her father's suicide in 1974. Her husband whipped out a twenty-dollar bill to donate to TheHopeLine. Their responses reminded me of the generous hearts of so many Americans, and that suicide of a loved one has left too many people scarred for life.

Meanwhile, Amy had been busy checking on ways for us to return to Massachusetts in the most economical way. Calling airlines and rental-car companies, she landed a one-way rental car in Williamsport, forty-five minutes away. Gary and Amy would drive us there. How could this couple—both working full-time, one with a school board meeting to prepare for and the other with a dissertation to write, and with three kids at home—drop everything for us on a Sunday? The sermon I had heard a couple of weeks earlier came to mind: *"You can't hurry and love at the same time!"* They were living out the sermon as they devoted their attention to our needs.

The pastor prayed for us before we departed to Gary and Amy's house. Jeff drove us there to swap vehicles with them so he could attend to matters at home. The grace, kindness, and care of these strangers overwhelmed us. With arrangements made for our trip back to Massachusetts, we headed to Williamsport to pick up the rental car.

Guardian angels Gary and Amy Martell on the left

My conversation with Amy on the way warmed my heart. I kept thanking her. With her wholesome smile looking me squarely in the face, she told me how pleased she was to be able to help us.

Later, after a late-night meal with them in Williamsport, she said, "My daily prayer to the Lord is, 'Bless me into usefulness.' He answered my prayer today through you."

> For He shall give His angels charge over you, to keep you in all your ways. In their hands they shall bear you up, lest you dash your foot against a stone.
>
> PSALM 91:11-12

Personal REFLECTION:

1. Do you believe God sends us helpers when we need them? When has He done this for you?

2. Have you ever been stunned by an unexpected set of circumstances, unable to move on? Who came to your aid?

3. When was the last time you felt an overwhelming urge to come to another person's aid? How do you think it made them feel?

EPILOGUE

The Ultimate Destination

What a ride! We're so glad you've landed here after covering parts of twenty-one US states, proving yet again that perseverance pays off. We hope the journey has been well worth the effort.

You've noticed Scripture references throughout this book as we aimed to bolster what we learned on the road with what the Bible has taught millions of seekers down through the ages. Before we pack up our gear and head home to catch up on mail and pay bills, we thought some of you might want to know what the Bible teaches about the ultimate destination. Pursuing that destination right now, if you're not already doing so, will allow you a leg up on many of the principles shared in this book.

Just as we move through our lives with side trips prompted by goals and endeavors tied to our individual passions and abilities, so too does everyone travel on a greater trip, one that includes this life and the life to come. You have a choice of two destinations, neither one of which will be in doubt when you die. Unlike our side trips, this journey's destination comes easily based upon one simple choice, and it's guaranteed. The choice is exclusively yours.

The two optional destinations of which we write are heaven and hell. Each has their attendant consequences in this life, too, but the stakes are much higher in the life to come.

The Bible says, "It is appointed for men to die once, but after this the judgment" (Hebrews 9:27). It also says, "For all have sinned and fall short of the glory of God" (Romans 3:23). How can any of us survive judgment by a holy, righteous God when our sin condemns us? Our sin resembles body odor or bad breath. We can clean it up or mask it, but eventually, it comes back to haunt us and those around us. Sin also acts like a ball and chain hooked to our foot as we walk around with a slow poison inside. It will entangle us and lead to our demise if we don't deal with it. Yet how do we rid ourselves of the effects of our own sin?

Well, there's good news! Even though our sin condemns us, God has made a provision for us. The Bible explains it this way: "For the wages of sin is death, but the gift of God is eternal life in Christ Jesus our Lord" (Romans 6:23). Yes, our sin filth comes with much more severe consequences than does our body stench. Yet God has made a way for us to get to Him: "But God demonstrates His own love toward us, in that while we were still sinners, Christ died for us" (Romans 5:8).

When Jesus came to Earth, fully man yet fully God, He lived a perfect, sinless life and taught us about spiritual truth. He also made some startling claims. Check this one out: "I am the way, the truth, and the life. No one comes to the Father except through Me" (John 14:6). He also said, "For God so loved the world that He gave His only begotten Son, that whoever believes in Him should not perish but have everlasting life" (John 3:16).

When Jesus died on the cross, He took all of our sins—past, present, and future—upon Himself. He died for our sins, for your sins, for the whole world's sins. When He died, He didn't just stay dead, which would have made Him no greater than any of the world's other great leaders, religious teachers, and prophets. No, Jesus came back to life, and many people saw Him before He ascended to heaven.

(Actually, over five hundred people saw the resurrected Jesus! See 1 Corinthians 15:3-8.) Now He sits at the right hand of the Father making the case for our forgiveness, because we can't do it on our own. In fact, we have no case apart from His sacrifice on our behalf. The blood that He shed on the cross pays the price for our sins. And His resurrection from the dead proves His claim that He was God in the flesh among us.

Just because Jesus died for our sins does not mean we will all go to heaven when we die. His death on the cross presents us with a choice. God is offering us a gift. And, like any gift, it is only complete when it is accepted. The Bible says, "But as many as received Him, to them He gave the right to become children of God" (John 1:12). To receive peace with God and eternal life with Him in heaven after you come to the end of your road on Earth, agree with God that you are a sinner in need of a savior and ask Him to forgive you. When you do, God will send His Holy Spirit to live inside of you. The Holy Spirit will help you know what God wants you to do. He'll place a strong sense of conviction about right and wrong within you, and He'll assure you of your salvation.

The Bible says, "that if you confess with your mouth the Lord Jesus and believe in your heart that God has raised Him from the dead, you will be saved. For with the heart one believes unto righteousness, and with the mouth confession is made unto salvation. For the Scripture says, 'Whoever believes on Him will not be put to shame.' For there is no distinction between Jew and Greek, for the same Lord over all is rich to all who call upon Him. For 'whoever calls on the name of the Lord shall be saved'" (Romans 10:9-13).

Are you ready to make peace with God right now? Simply speak to Him. Tell Him you're sorry for your sins and invite Him to come into your life, to make you the kind of person He wants you to be.

If you prayed that prayer, you've just made the most important decision of your life. Not only have you sealed your arrival at the ultimate destination when your body dies, you've also begun a life-transforming adventure. Congratulations! Share your decision with someone who will share in your joy. Over the next few weeks, read the Gospel of John from the Holy Bible to absorb just how much God loves you. Find some fellow Christians, perhaps at a local church, from whom you can receive encouragement and learn more about your newfound faith. Also, please send us a message using the contact form on the Open Road Press website to let us know about your good news. We'll be thrilled to hear it. God bless you, and happy trails through this life—and the next!

> There is therefore now no condemnation to those who are in Christ Jesus, who do not walk according to the flesh, but according to the Spirit. For the law of the Spirit of life in Christ Jesus has made me free from the law of sin and death.
>
> ROMANS 8:1-2

ACKNOWLEDGMENTS

No one can undertake cross-country bicycle touring without the help of others. The same can be said for a book project. It's difficult to explain the feeling when people give generously of their own time to help advance a project they believe is worthwhile. On this project, we had such contributions from family, friends, acquaintances, and total strangers—yet strangers no more! What better compliment and stronger encouragement can you give to two writers than to read their book, help them make it better, and tell others about it?

The following individuals and groups provided helpful critiques and direct contributions, bringing *Wheels of Wisdom* to fruition and launching it toward readers worldwide. We're deeply grateful.

Early reviewers: Jessica Bishop, Steve Bishop, David Harbison, Kaylea Harbison, Mary Harbison, Lynne Holmes, Jill Hoyt, Fred Ludwig, Kathy McHenry, Marilyn Sjoberg, Janet Timmins, and Sarah Williams.

Pre-publication reviewers: Tim Altman, Lance Barry, Karen Brits, Rick Cook, Peter DeHaan, Kolinda Duer, John Giannini, Lisa Lickel, Stacey Louiso-Henry, Tim Malikowski, Dan Miller, Tom Nenadal, Constance Rhodes, Jim Sayer, Ken Shirk, Patti Smith, Tim Streeter, Henk-Jan van der Klis, and Christian Women Affiliate's Unbound Crew, consisting of Heather Randall, Marisa Deshaies, Christie Hagerman, and Michelle Urdak.

Content, design, and editorial contributors: Dave Anderson, Erin Casey, GKS Creative, Micah Kandros, Aaron Kerr, John David Kudrick, Kathryn Lehan, Kevin Miller, and the Williamson County Public Library Critique Group. Thanks to the many others who helped us narrow down options for both the title and the cover.

ABOUT THE AUTHORS

Tim and Debbie Bishop have coauthored four books about their midlife launch into marriage, cross-country bicycle touring, and other matters of faith and inspiration. *Two Are Better: Midlife Newlyweds Bicycle Coast to Coast* captures the story behind the stories, while *Bicycle Touring How-To: What We Learned* shares their knowledge with bicycle touring wannabes. Now, *Wheels of Wisdom: Life Lessons for the Restless Spirit* conveys some deeper truths that apply to virtually any life pursuit. *Metaphors in Motion: Wisdom from the Open Road* is an e-book containing more lessons like those found in *Wheels of Wisdom*.

The Bishops serve as volunteer Hope Coaches for TheHopeLine, a nonprofit organization that seeks to reach, rescue, and restore hurting teens and young adults. They are available for speaking engagements about their touring and life experiences. They blog at http://www.openroadpress.com.

In addition to consulting for small businesses, Tim Bishop has written *Hedging Commodity Price Risk: A Small Business Perspective,* an e-book that explains hedging concepts in easy-to-understand language with practical examples. He has over thirty years of business experience and blogs on hedging at http://hedging.openroadpress.com.

Debbie Bishop has taught for over twenty-eight years. She has a passion for reading and seeing that young people do it well. She also has a strong interest in recovery issues and encouraging others with her own triumphs over such struggles earlier in her life. She is a featured author in *Love is Out There* by Melissa Williams-Pope, in which she relates her own story of finding love later than most. Debbie volunteers as a facilitator for www.findingbalance.com, an online support group dedicated to helping women who are struggling with eating disorders.

HOW TO HELP THEHOPELINE

thehopeline.com and 1-800-394-HOPE (4673)

Since TheHopeLine receives its support entirely from private sources, it is often in need of funding to sustain its important work. If you'd like to help TheHopeLine, you can pray for the organization and make a tax-deductible donation on its website at http://www.thehopeline.com/donate/.

TheHopeLine does life-changing work with downtrodden youth from ages thirteen to twenty-nine. Tim and Debbie Bishop have witnessed the difference that God's power and love have made in youth with whom they've interacted on TheHopeLine. They prepared a case for support (summarized below), which became part of their volunteer fundraising efforts on TheHopeLine Tour. You can read their entire case for support at http://www.openroadpress.com/links/thehopeline-tour-2014/why-support-thehopeline/.

1. TheHopeLine not only improves lives, it saves lives.

2. Your contribution to TheHopeLine helps make it free to the people who need it most.

3. TheHopeLine stands for clear thinking and right values.

4. TheHopeLine's efficient model maximizes the reach of your contribution dollar.

5. TheHopeLine is run with transparency and accountability.

6. TheHopeLine supports the mission of the church by reaching disconnected youth.

7. The testimonial evidence is compelling. Won't you support TheHopeLine today?

TheHopeLine is a service that seeks to reach, rescue, and restore hurting teens and young adults. Trained Hope Coaches handle phone calls and Internet chats from youth in crisis, and seek to listen, encourage, and, with permission, apply Scripture and pray for their issues. Hope Coaches also refer these youth to partner agencies that have expertise with issues like suicide, addiction, and abuse.

TheHopeLine, part of the Dawson McAllister Association, has transformed many lives since its inception in 1989. Although it deals with a wide array of youth issues, in each of the last three years the organization has intervened in the lives of over three thousand young people who were struggling with suicidal thoughts. Dawson McAllister, a dynamic youth speaker and author who has been in youth ministry since the 1970s, hosts two live, call-in radio shows to connect teens and young adults with the nonprofit's services. *DMLive* is syndicated on Top-40 stations nationwide. In February 2015, *TheHopeLine with Dawson McAllister* began airing on Christian radio stations. TheHopeLine's website streams its radio programming and offers a multitude of resources for healing hurts. The association partners with like-minded organizations that provide additional services, including counselors and e-mail mentors.

The Dawson McAllister Association is a 501(c)(3) organization in the United States of America. Any donations by US citizens are tax deductible to the fullest extent allowed by US law.

TRIP LOGS

10,527 MILES

31 STATES, 1 PROVINCE, AND THE DISTRICT OF COLUMBIA

210 TOTAL DAYS, 163 RIDING DAYS, 65 MILES PER DAY

TheHopeLine Tour (2014)

102 total days, 72 riding days, 14 states, 4,344 miles, 60 mpd

Date	Destination	Miles	Cum. Miles	Date	Destination	Miles	Cum. Miles
Starting in	Manzanita, OR						
July 3	Pacific City, OR	54	54	August 17	Sioux City, IA	44	2,296
July 4	Monmouth, OR	69	123	August 18-31	Sioux City, IA	Rest	
July 5	Springfield, OR	62	185	September 1	Onawa, IA	43	2,339
July 6-8	Springfield, OR	Rest		September 2	Council Bluffs, IA	67	2,406
July 9	Rainbow, OR	58	243	September 3	Nebraska City, NE	50	2,456
July 10	Redmond, OR	67	310	September 4	Falls City, NE	55	2,511
July 11	Mitchell, OR	68	378	September 5	Atchison, KS	60	2,571
July 12	John Day, OR	71	449	September 6	Holt, MO	64	2,635
July 13	Baker City, OR	83	532	September 7	Higginsville, MO	65	2,700
July 14	Baker City, OR	Rest		September 8	Higginsville, MO	Rest	
July 15	Oxbow, OR	70	602	September 9	Boonville, MO	78	2,778
July 16	Cambridge, ID	40	642	September 10	Boonville, MO	Rest	
July 17	Riggins, ID	81	723	September 11	Jefferson City, MO	60	2,838
July 18	Grangeville, ID	51	774	September 12	Washington, MO	80	2,918
July 19	Grangeville, ID	Rest		September 13	Sullivan, MO	33	2,951
July 20	Lowell, ID	47	821	September 14	Farmington, MO	60	3,011
July 21	Powell Junction, ID	66	887	September 15	Farmington, MO	Rest	
July 22	Missoula, MT	58	945	September 16	Cape Girardeau, MO	72	3,083
July 23	Missoula, MT	Rest		September 17	Metropolis, IL	72	3,155
July 24	Drummond, MT	60	1,005	September 18	Sturgis, KY	73	3,228
July 25	Anaconda, MT	58	1,063	September 19	Owensboro, KY	74	3,302
July 26	Whitehall, MT	45	1,108	September 20	Cloverport, KY	60	3,362
July 27	Belgrade, MT	69	1,177	September 21	Brandenburg, KY	38	3,400
July 28	Livingston, MT	44	1,221	September 22	Brandenburg, KY	Rest	
July 29	Columbus, MT	78	1,299	September 23	Sellersburg, IN	63	3,463
July 30	Columbus, MT	Rest		September 24	Carrollton, KY	61	3,524
July 31	Lovell, WY	85	1,384	September 25	Dry Ridge, KY	53	3,577
August 1	Worland, WY	71	1,455	September 26	Maysville, KY	68	3,645
August 2	Buffalo, WY	91	1,546	September 27	Milford, OH	70	3,715
August 3	Gillette, WY	75	1,621	September 28	Xenia, OH	54	3,769
August 4	Gillette, WY	Rest		September 29	Xenia, OH	Rest	
August 5	Upton, WY	48	1,669	September 30	Delaware, OH	79	3,848
August 6	Newcastle, WY	29	1,698	October 1	Bellville, OH	50	3,898
August 7	Keystone, SD	61	1,759	October 2	Medina, OH	73	3,971
August 8	Rapid City, SD	28	1,787	October 3-4	Medina, OH	Rest	
August 9	Interior, SD	80	1,867	October 5	Streetsboro, OH	34	4,005
August 10	Murdo, SD	77	1,944	October 6	Kinsman, OH	56	4,061
August 11	Murdo, SD	Rest		October 7	Meadville, PA	37	4,098
August 12	Oacoma, SD	71	2,015	October 8	Warren, PA	75	4,173
August 13	Platte, SD	50	2,065	October 9	Smethport, PA	56	4,229
August 14	Bonesteel, SD	44	2,109	October 10	Galeton, PA	49	4,278
August 15	Springfield, SD	80	2,189	October 11	Troy, PA	58	4,336
August 16	Vermillion, SD	63	2,252	October 12	East Troy, PA	8	4,344

Mom-to-Mom Tour (2012)
47 total days, 38 riding days, 14 states and DC, 2,654 miles, 70 mpd

Date	Destination	Miles	Cum. Miles	Date	Destination	Miles	Cum. Miles
Starting in	Naples, FL			August 3	Fredericksburg, VA	66	1,475
July 10	Port Charlotte, FL	70	70	August 4	Woodbridge, VA	51	1,526
July 11	Bowling Green, FL	51	121	August 5	Silver Spring, MD	56	1,582
July 12	Kissimmee, FL	86	207	August 6	Hunt Valley, MD	58	1,640
July 13	Mount Dora, FL	61	268	August 7	Columbia, PA	65	1,705
July 14	Ormond Beach, FL	85	353	August 8	Columbia, PA	Rest	
July 15-17	Ormond Beach, FL	Rest		August 9	Oaks, PA	80	1,785
July 18	St. Augustine, FL	58	411	August 10	Oaks, PA	Rest	
July 19	Yulee, FL	72	483	August 11	Easton, PA	87	1,872
July 20	Waycross, GA	67	550	August 12	Del. Water Gap, PA	31	1,903
July 21	Statesboro, GA	102	652	August 13	New Paltz, NY	92	1,995
July 22	Statesboro, GA	Rest		August 14	Norfolk, CT	64	2,059
July 23	Yemassee, SC	78	730	August 15	East Windsor, CT	44	2,103
July 24	Moncks Corner, SC	79	809	August 16	Sutton, MA	73	2,176
July 25	Conway, SC	89	898	August 17	Marlborough, MA	35	2,211
July 26	Shallotte, NC	54	952	August 18-19	Marlborough, MA	Rest	
July 27	Wilmington, NC	69	1,021	August 20	Exeter, NH	85	2,296
July 28	New Bern, NC	93	1,114	August 21	Windham, ME	91	2,387
July 29	New Bern, NC	Rest		August 22	Rockport, ME	89	2,476
July 30	Plymouth, NC	72	1,186	August 23	Bangor, ME	59	2,535
July 31	Suffolk, VA	91	1,277	August 24	Lincoln, ME	49	2,584
August 1	Williamsburg, VA	55	1,332	August 25	Houlton, ME	70	2,654
August 2	Ashland, VA	77	1,409				

Honeymoon on Wheels (2010)
61 total days, 53 riding days, 15 states and 1 province, 3,529 miles, 67 mpd

Date	Destination	Miles	Cum. Miles	Date	Destination	Miles	Cum. Miles
Starting in	Seaside, OR			August 4	Foreston, MN	69	1,877
July 3	Westport, OR	47	47	August 5	Shuttle: Wabasha, MN	Rest	
July 4	Portland, OR	72	119	August 6	Winona, MN	40	1,917
July 5	Cascade Locks, OR	55	174	August 7	Shuttle: Cascade, IA	Rest	
July 6	Biggs, OR	66	240	August 8	Wilton, IA	61	1,978
July 7	Crow Butte, WA	57	297	August 9	Kewanee, IL	90	2,068
July 8	Umatilla, OR	37	334	August 10	Streator, IL	69	2,137
July 9	Walla Walla, WA	54	388	August 11	Kankakee, IL	70	2,207
July 10	Clarkston, WA	96	484	August 12	Rensselaer, IN	53	2,260
July 11	Culdesac, ID	40	524	August 13	Wabash, IN	87	2,347
July 12	Kamiah, ID	54	578	August 14	Monroeville, IN	60	2,407
July 13	Clearwater Nat For, ID	55	633	August 15	Napoleon, OH	67	2,474
July 14	Lolo Hot Springs, MT	60	693	August 16	Milan, OH	94	2,568
July 15	Missoula, MT	38	731	August 17	Cleveland, OH	51	2,619
July 16	Lincoln, MT	78	809	August 18	Cleveland, OH	Rest	
July 17	Great Falls, MT	88	897	August 19	Conneaut, OH	91	2,710
July 18-21	Great Falls, MT	Rest		August 20	Westfield, NY	67	2,777
July 22	Fort Benton, MT	55	952	August 21	Hamburg, NY	62	2,839
July 23	Havre, MT	73	1,025	August 22	Niagara Falls, ON	45	2,884
July 24	Malta, MT	88	1,113	August 23	Medina, NY	49	2,933
July 25	Glasgow, MT	70	1,183	August 24	Egypt, NY	61	2,994
July 26	Poplar, MT	71	1,254	August 25	Fulton, NY	78	3,072
July 27	Williston, ND	81	1,335	August 26	Redfield, NY	47	3,119
July 28	Shuttle: Minot, ND	Rest		August 27	Raquette Lake, NY	79	3,198
July 29	Rugby, ND	60	1,395	August 28	Ticonderoga, NY	86	3,284
July 30	Carrington, ND	98	1,493	August 29	Middlebury, VT	25	3,309
July 31	Mayville, ND	93	1,586	August 30	Fairlee, VT	75	3,384
August 1	Fargo, ND	60	1,646	August 31	Conway, NH	77	3,461
August 2	Fergus Falls, MN	79	1,725	September 1	Cape Elizabeth, ME	68	3,529
August 3	Long Prairie, MN	83	1,808				

TOPICAL INDEX

GEOGRAPHICAL INDEX

LEGEND:

HW = 2010 HONEYMOON ON WHEELS

MMT = 2012 MOM-TO-MOM TOUR

HLT = THEHOPELINE TOUR OF 2014

LESSON NUMBER IN PARENTHESES